The caption on this public information photo, dated
declares that the gathering was taken at: "a facto
[Lancasters] are produced in surprising numbe
Production". Left to right: G Philip Andrews,
'Air Tech' of New York City; Thomas Mart
at Waterton, New York; Avro test pilc
editor of 'Industry and Power', S
his time as a test pilot with
Orrell clocked up 8,174 h,
types. He piloted 917 different Lancasters, nearly
a quarter of those built at Woodford.
VIA DEAN WRIGHT

CONTENTS

FRONT COVER
The Battle of Britain Memorial Flight Mk.I PA474 in the colours of 100 Squadron's EE139 'Phantom of the Ruhr' – a veteran of 121 'ops' with 100 and 550 Squadrons.
For more on the 'Phantom', see page 52. JOHN M DIBBS - PLANE PICTURE COMPANY

THIS PAGE
Sheer, unforgettable magic was made in 2014 when the Canadian Warplane Heritage Mk.X flew in British skies with the Battle of Britain Memorial Flight Mk.I PA474.
For more on both of these machines, see page 28. DARREN HARBAR

Edited by: **Ken Ellis** With thanks to: **Chris Gilson, Steve Beebee, Jeremy Brooks, Sue Campbell, Darren Harbar**
Group Editor: **Nigel Price**

Art Editor: **Mike Carr**
Chief Designer: **Steve Donovan**

Production Editor: **Sue Blunt**
Deputy Production Editor: **Carol Randall**
Production Manager: **Janet Watkins**

Advertisement Manager: **Alison Sanders**
Advertising Production: **Debi McGowan**
Group Advertisement Manager: **Brodie Baxter**

Marketing Executive: **Shaun Binnington**
Marketing Manager: **Martin Steele**

Commercial Director: **Ann Saundry**
Managing Director and Publisher: **Adrian Cox**
Executive Chairman: **Richard Cox**

Contacts
Key Publishing Ltd, PO Box 100, Stamford, Lincs, PE9 1XQ
Tel 01780 755131
Email flypast@keypublishing.com
www.keypublishing.com

Distribution: **Seymour Distribution Ltd**, 2 Poultry Avenue, London EC1A 9PP. Tel 020 74294000

Printed by: **Warners (Midland) plc**, The Maltings, Bourne, Lincs, PE10 9PH

Published by: **Key Publishing Ltd** – see above
Printed in England

BIPLANE TO DEL

ROY CHADWICK, THE MAN WHO DESIGNED THE
LANCASTER, TOOK AVRO FROM BIPLANE TRAINERS TO
NUCLEAR BOMBERS. KEN ELLIS EXPLAINS

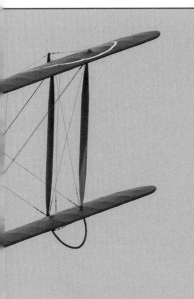

etween Bolton and Manchester is Farnworth in what was then lush Lancashire countryside; Roy Chadwick was born there on April 30, 1893. By the age of 11 he was building and flying intricate model aircraft. Three years later Roy was employed as a trainee draughtsman at an engineering firm.

On July 13, 1909 Manchester-born Alliott Verdon Roe, a one-time prize-winning aero modeller, became the first person to fly an all-British aeroplane – his Triplane that today takes pride of place in London's Science Museum.

Trading under the name A V Roe and Company, or simply Avro, Roe had a workshop at Brownsfield Mill in Manchester's Ancoats district. In July 1910 young Roy peeked inside where frail triplanes and biplanes were being created. Later that month, Roy joined the huge crowds attending the second Blackpool Aviation Meeting where Roe and others were flying.

Afterwards Roy could think of nothing else. Surely there was employment to be had for an aircraft mad, trained draughtsman from this inspiring pioneer aviator, fellow modeller and Lancastrian? Approaching his 18th birthday, Roy took the plunge and asked the great man – 16 years his senior – for a job. Roe said yes, and from that day the prospects for the lad from Farnworth, Avro and British aviation were transformed.

Eccles for its maiden flight. Enquiries with Parky produced a 'nod' and Roy climbed into the front seat. A swift circuit was followed by a bounce on landing and the biplane ended up on its nose. Pilot and aspirant designer were unhurt. Roy had tasted flight.

Manufacture of the 504 ran throughout the Great War and well beyond with many sub-variants, licence production, exports and rebuilds. The 'second-generation' 504N extended the design into the 1930s. Just how many 504s were built across the world is a matter of debate, but it's in the region of 10,000.

CLOSE SHAVE

During the war Roy's fertile mind turned to bombers and fighters, including the twin-engined Pike and Manchester biplanes, but these achieved only meagre orders. In 1917, Avro expanded into a purpose-built factory at Hamble in Hampshire and Roy presided over the extensive drawing office there. That year the 24-year-old was appointed chief designer.

Lucrative though the 504 family was, Avro needed to diversify. With a 68ft (20.7m) span the single-engined Aldershot day bomber of 1922 was massive. Fifteen were ordered by the RAF, just sufficient

SETTING THE STANDARD

Among Roy's first work, under Roe's guidance, was a detailed rethink of the Type E 'Military Biplane' which had been first flown by Wilfred 'Parky' Parke in March 1912. Practical, and with great potential, it was rebranded as the Type 500 and formed the basis of the famous Avro 504. This exceptional biplane set the standard for trainers for decades hence, and turned Avro from a hand-to-mouth workshop into an industry.

Roy was itching to get airborne, but most of the early machines had just one seat. The Type 500 was a two-seater and even offered then revolutionary dual control. Here was his chance to experience the end-product of his drawings and calculations.

In July 1912 the third Type 500 was taken from Brownsfield Mill to the cricket pitch at

for 99 Squadron, but that was a typical purchase by the Air Ministry in the cash-strapped 1920s and early 1930s. ⊕

"THE BREAKTHROUGH CAME WHEN AVRO RESPONDED TO AN IMPERIAL AIRWAYS REQUIREMENT FOR A PAIR TWIN-ENGINED LUXURY CHARTER AIRCRAFT. ...ROY'S MULTI-PURPOSE ANSON RAN FOR 17 YEARS AND 11,020 UNITS, THROUGH AN INCREDIBLE NUMBER OF VARIANTS, WITH EXTENSIVE EXPORTS AND LICENCES."

Roe was determined to break into light aviation and Roy's first foray in that direction was the single-seat Baby sports biplane. Occasionally test piloting at Hamble was Harold Hamersley and one of his tasks was to teach Roy to fly.

On the last day of April 1919 Harold took the prototype Baby for its maiden flight. At about 300ft he accidently knocked off the ignition switches and the little 35hp (26kW) engine stopped; the Baby entered a spin and splattered into the mud of the River Hamble.

Harold was not sent packing; he successfully flew the second Baby on May 10. Roy flew this machine frequently, but it nearly brought a dazzling career to an abrupt end on January 13, 1920. In a website devoted to her father, Margaret Dove (who died in 2008) described what happened: "Roy had gone up without his flying jacket. It was a cold day, and he fainted. He came to as he was crashing into trees beside the aerodrome. His right arm, left leg and pelvis were severely fractured and the joystick went through his neck! He later made a full recovery, thanks to the skill of the great World War One surgeon, Sir Arbuthnot Lane."

For Avro, the real

step forward in light aeroplanes came in 1926 with the first Avian two-seat tourer/trainer. It was not to rival de Havilland's exceptional Moth dynasty, but it did enter volume production.

BREAKTHROUGH ANSON

In 1930 the first Tutor flew; the summation of all Roy's experience of what a military trainer should be. Like the 504, other variants were offered, including the less complex Cadet and Prefect, and once again there were exports and licence agreements to swell the coffers.

Niche markets like trainers were all very well, but more complex military roles offered the greatest growth potential. The breakthrough came when Avro responded to an Imperial Airways requirement for a twin-engined luxury charter aircraft. The sleek, retractable undercarriage monoplane, the Type 652, translated with ease into a maritime patroller for the RAF; both versions flew in 1935.

The Anson emulated the success and fame of its 504 forebear and Avro became a production giant. Manufacture of Roy's multi-purpose Anson ran for 17 years and 11,020 units, through an incredible number of variants, with extensive exports and licences. Avro was now ready to pitch for the bomber contracts that were looming as Britain geared up for another European war.

The feature *Two to Four* on page 10 covers the first steps to the Lancaster, while *Legacy*, page 94 takes the story to the York transport, the Lincoln and beyond.

Experience with the York and the Lancastrian encouraged Avro to enter the post-war airliner market and the result was the elegant-looking Tudor 1 for British Overseas Airways Corporation (BOAC). 'Bill' Thorn took the prototype, G-AGPF, for its first flight at Woodford, Manchester, in June 1945. Two years later BOAC abandoned the Tudor 1.

In parallel with the Tudor 1, BOAC requested the high-capacity Tudor 2. With a fuselage length of 105ft 7in it was the longest British aircraft at the time. Bill captained the prototype, G-AGSU, in May 1946.

TRAGEDY

On August 23, 1947 Bill prepared to take *Sugar-Uncle* for a test with a crew of three and a trio of keen passengers: Roy; Stuart Davies, Chadwick's nominated successor; and Sir Roy Dobson, the company's indomitable boss. An important telephone call pulled Dobson away and the sortie continued without him. As the airliner climbed it banked violently to starboard and cartwheeled; the fuselage broke in two places and the wreck plummeted into a large pond.

Miraculously, flight-test engineer Eddie Talbot and Stuart Davies survived. Bill and Sqn Ldr David Wilson drowned in the cockpit; Roy and radio operator John Webster were both thrown clear and died of fractured skulls.

During maintenance, G-AGSU's ailerons had been rigged wrongly – starboard down on the control wheel produced 'up' and the opposite to port. Before he could establish this cross-over, Bill's control inputs put the Tudor into an ever-deepening roll.

The long fuselage meant that a visual check from the cockpit to see that the ailerons were working as they should be was not possible; this could only be done with help from ground crew physically indicating 'starboard aileron down' etc. It was a salutary lesson in pre-flight procedure with large aeroplanes.

Everyone at Woodford was stunned; the loss of the flight crew was terrible enough, but Roy was synonymous with Avro – a giant of his time. Among Chadwick's last work had been overseeing mock-ups for the up-coming Shackleton maritime patroller and sketches confirming the delta configuration of what would become the Vulcan.

TRIBUTE

By far and away the best tribute is *Architect of Wings – A Biography of Roy Chadwick, Designer of the Lancaster Bomber* by Harald Penrose, published in 1985. Anyone who calls themselves a fan of the Lancaster needs to have read this detailed and loving tome.

There is no better way to conclude this fleeting testament to Roy Chadwick CBE than through the words of Harald: "His inspiration lived on. The designs of the Athena trainer, Coastal Command Shackleton, Tudor development into the jet-powered Ashton, and the thunderous long-serving Vulcan bomber were completed in due course by Stuart Davies. To this day the surviving pilots who flew the wartime Lancasters speak of their machines with nostalgic admiration, and regard Roy Chadwick as the greatest aircraft designer of all." ●

CLOCKWISE FROM TOP LEFT
Hinkler with Avro designer Roy Chadwick on his right and general manager Reginald Parrott to his left in front of Avian G-EBOV at Hamble, Hampshire, prior to Bert's epic flight to Australia in 1928. BRITISH AEROSPACE

A total of 10,996 examples of the exceptional Anson were built 1936 to 1952: Mk.I of 1938 illustrated. AVRO

The huge Tudor 2 prototype at Woodford, 1946. KEY COLLECTION

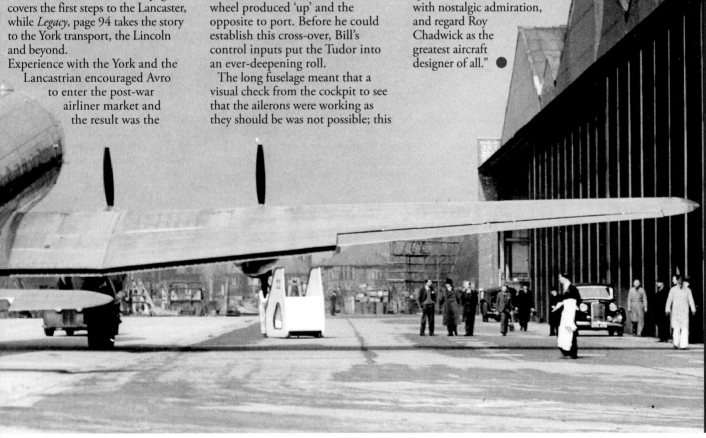

TWO TO

BELOW
Manchester I L7515 of 207 Squadron having fun with an HP Hampden acting as a photo-ship in November 1941.
ALL KEY COLLECTION
UNLESS NOTED

It was not enough to request a state-of-the-art twin-engined bomber to radically enhance Bomber Command's 'punch'. An invitation to tender was sent out to the British aircraft industry on September 8, 1936 – just two months after the new strike force came into being.

The statistics were challenging; the winning design was to carry up to 8,000lb of bombs at no less than 275mph (442km/h) for a maximum range of 2,000 miles (3,218km). But Air Ministry specification P13/36 wanted much more of the RAF's next spearhead.

In order to use existing airfields while carrying the greatest weapon load, the bomber had to be stressed to use a catapult launch system to hurl it into the air. It would also be called upon to serve as a torpedo bomber, with a pair of 18in (45cm) 'tin fish' carried internally. To increase the accuracy of weapon aiming and reduce time over the target, it should be capable of dive attacks at 60°. Use in the general reconnaissance – maritime patrol – role with minimal equipment changes was to be possible. Oh, and the ability to transport 16 fully equipped troops long distances was also requested.

Avro, Boulton Paul, Bristol, Handley Page, Shorts and Vickers were all asked to see what they could come up with to meet P13/36. With a European war very much on the cards, lucrative contracts awaited, but such a demanding 'shopping list' made the venture extremely high risk.

Avro at Woodford, Manchester, and Handley Page (HP) of Radlett, Hertfordshire, were awarded contracts to build prototypes. The end products would be named Manchester and Halifax respectively.

GREATEST HURDLE

In terms of aerodynamics, construction techniques, armament and hundreds of other aspects, P13/36 was an awesome commission. By far and away the greatest hurdle was the powerplant; the design teams at Woodford (Avro) and Radlett (HP) both opted for the projected Vulture from Rolls-Royce (RR).

Building on the technology of the Kestrel and Peregrine V-format 12-cylinder series, RR intended to create a relatively compact engine that could belt out 1,800hp (1,342kW). Essentially, the Vulture was a pair of Peregrines on a common crankshaft and crankcase with a supercharger – it was a 24-cylinder, X-format brute.

With one, possibly two, bombers fitted with Vultures and Hawker and Vickers planning to use the engine for, respectively, the Tornado fighter and the Warwick bomber, RR faced potentially a massive marketplace. (The Tornado did not enter production and the Warwick eventually settled for radials.)

It was 1939 before a heavily modified Hawker Henley test-bed got a Vulture airborne; too late to prevent the Air Ministry from instructing HP to redesign its proposal to take four RR Merlins. Avro, which had been given an off-the-drawing-board production order in July 1937, was told to stick with the Vulture.

DELAYED AND OVERWEIGHT

Under the leadership of incredibly gifted designer Roy Chadwick, the Manchester took shape. (See *Biplane to Delta* on page 6 for more on Chadwick.) Gradually all of the non-bomber requirements for P13/36 were dropped; bizarrely the last to go was the troop-carrying role. As the design had long since been 'frozen', many elements of the original specification had to stay in place, with weight penalties.

But some of P13/36's latent demands played a major part in making the Manchester's successor, the Lancaster, a war-winner. The torpedo requirement necessitated a huge bomb bay that would go on to carry a 'bouncing' bomb or the 22,000lb (9.979kg) Tallboy 'earthquake' weapon. To be able to accommodate soldiers, the fuselage had to be broad and deep, helping to make the Lancaster versatile when it came to internal equipment changes. This also made the post-war airliner version, the Lancastrian, possible.

Ease of production and maintenance was stipulated by P13/36. Chadwick created a modular airframe that permitted

FOUR

major sections to be manufactured off-site by sub-contractors. This also meant damaged Lancasters could be dismantled and returned by road for rebuild.

At Derby, RR was swamped by demands for Merlins for Hurricanes, Spitfires, Beaufighters and Halifaxes. The Vulture became long-delayed and over budget. Despite a series of 'fixes' it remained unreliable and – in the minds of many Manchester crews – downright dangerous. When it was axed, fewer than 600 units had been built and the Avro twin was the only type to take it on operations.

NIGHTMARE

Today it is Manchester Airport, but on July 25, 1939 the airfield was known as Ringway, the flight test centre for Avro. Like its powerplant, the prototype Manchester, L7246, was also behind schedule and on that day chief test pilot Harry Albert 'Sam' Brown and co-pilot Sidney Albert 'Bill' Thorn took

the eagerly anticipated bomber up for its maiden flight.

Performance was way below what was hoped for, the Vultures laboured throughout the flight and directional stability was poor. A small, shark-like, fin on the upper rear fuselage, quickly replaced by a more conventional design, helped improve the latter.

A pressing need was to get the prototype evaluated by the Aeroplane and Armament Experimental Establishment at Boscombe Down, Wiltshire. There was to be

an agonising delay until the second example, L7247, joined the programme, on May 26,

1940. Thorn set out from Woodford on November 29, 1939 to deliver L7246 to Boscombe Down, it was the start of a nightmare. The port Vulture cut out and Thorn managed a force landing near Market Drayton, Shropshire. In fairness to the engine, a fuel-tank selection glitch was to blame. It was Brown's turn to ferry the repaired aircraft to ⏩

"USE IN THE MARITIME PATROL ROLE WITH MINIMAL EQUIPMENT CHANGES WAS TO BE POSSIBLE. OH, AND THE ABILITY TO TRANSPORT 16 FULLY EQUIPPED TROOPS LONG DISTANCES WAS ALSO REQUESTED."

the Manchester was a viable war machine. Diversions to create a Mk.II with exceptionally complex armament options did not help; this was thankfully cancelled in June 1940. From the maiden flight to mid-1940 the Manchester had increased in weight by more than 4,500lb.

Throwing the towel in was not an option. While the Anson was a spectacular production success, if the Manchester failed, in the medium term Avro faced a future as a sub-contractor for others.

Despite all the odds, fourth production example L7279 was issued to 207 Squadron at Waddington, Lincolnshire, on November 6, 1940. Four days previously 35 Squadron at Leeming in Yorkshire took delivery of its first operational Halifax, powered by four Merlins.

Wisely, Chadwick had been looking at powerplant options. Staying with a twin format, there was the Bristol Centaurus and the Napier Sabre, but both were in their earliest stages. If four engines were required, the radial Hercules or Taurus from Bristol might suffice, but the Merlin dominated.

On April 18, 1940 Avro proposed the bigger-winged Manchester III with four Merlins. That

Boscombe on December 10. Two days later, on take-off at 300ft a Vulture failed and L7246 ended up on its belly. Repairs were swift but on December 23 *another* Vulture packed up, this time at 3,000ft. The prototype slithered to a halt in a field not far from Boscombe. It was returned to Woodford – in a convoy of lorries – for rebuild.

As RR struggled with the Vulture, Chadwick's team faced endless redesigns, changes in systems and fittings in an attempt to prove that

month Stuart 'Cock' Davies was appointed as head of the Experimental Department to oversee the project. This crucial task was pivotal to the 34-year-old's career.

As work to refine the Mk.III continued, this was a nail-biting time for Avro. In November 1940 the Ministry of Aircraft Production gave consideration to switching the Avro and Metropolitan-Vickers assembly lines to churning out Halifaxes. Thankfully it was more efficient to introduce the Manchester III than stop everything and re-jig for the HP bomber, so approval was given to go ahead.

Chadwick's basic design was sound and a weight-reduction scheme coupled with operational experience meant that the Merlin-powered version was a giant leap on from its predecessor.

NAME CHANGE

The alterations were so comprehensive and as the Manchester 'brand' was hardly bathed in glory, a name-change was needed. On December 28, 1940 the prototype Mk.III, BT308, had its first engine runs at Ringway. Chadwick signed its clearance to fly on January 5, 1941 and the document referred to BT308 not as a Manchester III, but a Lancaster.

Four days later the same pilots that took the Manchester skyward for the first time – Brown and Thorn – carried out the maiden flight of the Lancaster. Forty minutes later BT308 returned; its pilots very happy. The trip to Boscombe Down was made – uneventfully – on January 27 and BT308 was generally well greeted.

It was given a fixed middle fin, Manchester-style, but on February 21 flew with a wider tailplane and larger twin fins and rudders.

The second prototype, DG595, was first flown on May 13, 1941. It was built to full production standard – the changeover from Manchester to Lancaster was to be as seamless as possible. The Vulture was cancelled in September 1941 and the last Manchester, R5841, was issued for service in March of the following year.

RENOWNED FOR BOMBERS

The Lancaster transformed the prospects for Avro. Previously known more for trainers, the company became renowned for bombers, culminating in the phenomenal Vulcan. The delta was designed by the man who had nurtured the Lancaster, Stuart Davies

That very first 'Lanc' worked hard. In September 1941 BT308 was sent

to Waddington where it was used for service trials and crew familiarisation. Teams from the resident 207 Squadron, still flying Manchesters; 44 Squadron with HP Hampdens and the Manchester-equipped 97 Squadron at nearby Coningsby, all received their first taste of the future from BT308.

After that it served on trials with RR before joining the trials fleet of the Royal Aircraft Establishment at Farnborough, Hampshire. In January 1943 BT308 was ferried to Coventry where Armstrong Whitworth converted it into a test-bed for the next generation, fitting a Metropolitan-Vickers F2/1 turbojet into the rear fuselage.

The five-engined BT308 had its last flight on July 20, 1944 and was retired. There was a war on and no space for sentiment so this outstanding prototype was destined for the breaker's yard. ●

BUILDING A
LEGEND

DANIEL FORD DESCRIBES THE TRANSATLANTIC INDUSTRY THAT
MANUFACTURED LANCASTERS

From the beginning the Manchester, and is successor, the Lancaster, were composed of sub-assemblies, even the largest of which could be moved by road with relative ease. The main Avro factory was at Chadderton in north Manchester, while the assembly line and flight test airfield was at Woodford, to the south of the city.

This modular construction also facilitated sub-contracting to other concerns, permitting wide dispersal of factories and workshops, and in turn making it harder for the Luftwaffe to interrupt production.

Once in service, this method of construction allowed for replacement and repair of even large sections. Furthermore, when the time came for major overhaul, or repair, the bombers could

be dismantled and trucked to contractors.

Production of the Manchester twin-engined bomber was established by Avro from Chadderton, quickly followed by Metropolitan-Vickers at Trafford Park. Both organisations supplied the final assembly tracks at Woodford.

MOTOR TRADE

In Birmingham, vehicle mass manufacturing skills were applied to producing the bomber. Austin Motors at Longbridge, and the massive Castle Bromwich Aircraft Factory, originally established by Morris Motors, both built Lancasters. 'Castle Brom' was managed by Vickers-Armstrongs from the spring of 1940 and the latter also established an assembly line at Hawarden,

near Chester, which initially made Wellingtons.

Avro became a member of the Hawker Siddeley group of companies, headed by Thomas Sopwith, in 1935. Another part of the combine was Armstrong Whitworth and that organisation became the second-largest Lancaster constructor at its sites at Baginton and Bitteswell. (See the panel overleaf for more.)

From Chadderton and its associated sub-factories, Avro produced a total of 3,673 Lancasters, with final assembly and flight test at Woodford and Yeadon. The Woodford plant boasted three production lines, each a quarter of a mile long. Ignoring Metropolitan-Vickers output, in August 1944 Woodford churned out 155 'pure' *Avro* Lancasters – an incredible achievement. ➔

BELOW
The final assembly line at Armstrong Whitworth, Bitteswell. To the right is Mk.I LM296 which was delivered to 50 Squadron at Skellingthorpe in the spring of 1944, serving as 'T-for-Tare'. KEC

"THIS MODULAR CONSTRUCTION ALSO FACILITATED SUB-CONTRACTING TO OTHER CONCERNS, PERMITTING WIDE DISPERSAL OF FACTORIES AND WORKSHOPS, AND IN TURN MAKING IT HARDER FOR THE LUFTWAFFE TO INTERRUPT PRODUCTION."

Lancaster nose sections at the huge Avro plant at Chadderton, Manchester.
BRITISH AEROSPACE

LANCASTER VARIANTS

Mk.I — Initial production version. Sub-variants included the Mk.I (Special) that could take the 'Tallboy' and 'Grand Slam' high-capacity bombs; the Mk.I (FE) modified for the Far East with 'Tiger Force'; and the post-war PR.1 photo-survey conversion

Mk.II — As Mk.I but powered by Bristol Hercules radials

Mk.III — As Mk.I but with Packard-built Merlins. The aircraft modified to take the 'Upkeep' 'bouncing bomb' were known as Mk.III (Provisioning). Coastal Command conversions were the ASR.III (ASR.3 from 1948) for air-sea rescue and GR.III and MR.III for general reconnaissance and maritime reconnaissance respectively

Mk.IV and V — Initial designations for the Lincoln I and II

Mk.VI — Higher-powered version with Merlin 85s and annular cowlings, eight completed

Mk.VII — Produced by Austin with Martin-built top turret. Also Mk.VII (FE) with mods for the Far East with 'Tiger Force'

Mk.VIII and IX — Not built

Mk.X — Production by Victory Aircraft in Canada, with Packard-built Merlins for Bomber Command. Post-war use by the RCAF, aircraft were designated Mk.10 with mission prefixes, eg 10-MR maritime reconnaissance and 10-DC drone launcher

A Lancaster under final assembly at Bitteswell, early 1944. KEC

At Castle Bromwich, a vast area was used to store finished parts and sub-assemblies, either fabricated on site or by sub-contractors, until they were needed on the assembly line. KEC

The centre section, inner wings and inboard engine/undercarriage fairings sub-assembly was one of the bulkiest items, but still readily transportable by road. Illustrated are examples at Castle Bromwich awaiting their turn on the assembly line. KEC

Press cutting from the launch of Leicester's ambitious Lancaster Fund, 1943. An appropriately named target board was erected outside the town hall showing the German cities of Essen, Hanover and Berlin. A Lancaster outline was added every time sufficient money had been collected to acquire an example. The purchase of 100 bombers was given as £2,097,678 – in present day values just shy of a staggering £160 million – and was achieved. Ventures like this were run all over the UK and Commonwealth. KEC

The Lancaster repair and refurbishing line run by Tollerton Aircraft Services at Tollerton, Nottingham, 1945. In the foreground are Mk.Is ED866 and LM420, both of which carry the markings of the Syerston-based 5 Lancaster Finishing School. As related in the feature '75 Lancs', starting on page 28, ED866 became civil registered with Flight Refuelling as G-AHJW, but met with tragedy in 1948. KEC

LANCASTER PRODUCTION CENTRES

AVRO

Main factory Chadderton, Manchester; assembly and flight test at Woodford, Manchester, from October 1941. Production at Yeadon, Yorkshire, from November 1942,
Prototypes BT308, DG595 and DT810, followed by Mk.Is and Mk.IIIs: L7527 to L7584, R5482 to R5763, W4102 to W4384, ED303 to ED999, EE105 to EE202, JA672 to JA981, JB113 to JB748, LM301 to LM756, ME295 to ME551, ND324 to ND996, NE112 to NE181, PA964 to PA999, PB112 to PB998, PD112 to PD196, RE115 to RE226, SW319 to SW377, TX263 to TX273

Total constructed at both sites 3,673, last built - at Yeadon - October 1945

ARMSTRONG WHITWORTH

Main factory Whitley, Warwickshire. Assembly and flight test at Sywell, Northampton, August 1942 to late 1943; Baginton, Coventry, from 1942; Bitteswell, Leicestershire, from 1944.
Mk.Is, Mk.IIs and Mk.IIIs: DS601 to DS852, LL617 to LL977, LM100 to LM296, NF906 to NF999, NG113 to NG503, RF120 to RF326, SW283 to SW316, TW647 to TW911

Production completed in March 1946. Total built: 1,329

AUSTIN

Austin Aero, a division of Austin Motors. Factory, assembly and flight test at Longbridge, Birmingham.
Mk.Is and Mk.VIIs: NN694 to NN816, NX548 to NX794, RT670 to RT750

From March 1944 to January 1946, construction totalled 330

METROPOLITAN-VICKERS

Main factory at Trafford Park, Manchester; assembly and flight test at Woodford, from January 1942. From June to August 1945, assembly and flight test at Hawarden, Chester.
Mk.Is and Mk.IIIs: R5842 to R5917, W4761 to W5012, DV155 to DV407, ME554 to ME868, PD198 to PD444, RA500 to RA806, SW243 to SW279, TW915 to TW929

Total production 1,080

VICKERS-ARMSTRONGS

Factory, assembly and flight test at Castle Bromwich, Birmingham. Built 300 from November 1943 to August 1945.
Mk.Is: HK535 to HK806, PP663 to PP792
Assembly and flight test at Hawarden, Chester, from June 1944 to September 1945 - constructed 235
Mk.Is: PA158 to PA509

VICTORY AIRCRAFT

Factory, assembly and flight at Malton, Ontario, Canada. From September 1943 to May 1945 - built 430. (Company became Avro Canada in 1945.)
Mk.Xs: KB700 to KB999, FM100 to FM229 in that order

Note: Serial number batches are quoted from first to last, but for space purposes exclude 'black out' blocks. Readers will be able to use this guide to establish where a particular Lancaster was made.

DEBUT

ANDREW THOMAS TELLS THE STORY OF THE
LANCASTER'S INTRODUCTION TO RAF SERVICE WITH 44
SQUADRON AT WADDINGTON

Seventy-five years ago the Lancaster went to war for the first time. After the failure of the twin-engined Manchester, much was expected of the new Avro type by the recently appointed Bomber Command leader, AM Sir Arthur Harris. The Lancaster was not going to let him down.

It was on Christmas Eve 1941 that the men of 44 Squadron at Waddington, near Lincoln, received an early present when the first three Lancasters were delivered. Led by Wg Cdr Roderick Leoroyd VC, the unit had been selected as the first to receive Bomber Command's latest weapon.

Previously equipped with twin-engined Handley Page Hampdens, training on the complex new type began immediately. Additional aircrew were posted in to 44 Sqn as the Lancaster carried seven while the Hampden only had four.

Bomber Command was keen to see its latest type committed to action and, from late January 1942, the squadron stood by several times – but weather or other reasons caused cancellations.

Eventually, on the evening of March 3, watched by AVM John Slessor, the Air Officer Commanding 5 Group, four Lancasters flown by Sqn Ldr John Nettleton, Flt Lt Sandford and W/Os Crum and Lamb lifted off from Waddington to lay mines in the waters of the Heligoland Bight, off the mouth of the River Elbe on Germany's northwest coast. All four returned after the uneventful debut.

Working up continued apace and on the night of March 10/11 two aircraft from the squadron joined 41 Vickers Wellingtons, seven Short Stirlings and three Manchesters in a raid on Essen – the Lancaster's first true bombing operation.

On March 24, F/Sgt Lyster Warren-Smith and his crew set out to lay mines off the French port of Lorient. Believed to have been a victim of German flak, *M-for-Mother* became the first Lancaster to fail to return from operations. All eight of its crew, including a 'second dickie' pilot, perished.

LOW LEVEL IN DAYLIGHT

Allied shipping losses in the Atlantic reached horrific levels in the early months of 1942 and it became a strategic priority to reduce the U-boat threat by all available means. Bomber Command was requested to deal with a factory making submarine diesel engines at Augsburg in Bavaria.

To ensure accuracy, the plan called for a low-level attack in daylight using the RAF's latest bomber. It was breathtakingly audacious, involving an unescorted round trip of more than 1,000 miles (1,609km), most of it over enemy territory.

Six Lancasters each from 44 and 97 Squadrons would take part in the raid. In early April long-range low-level formation training began on routes around Britain, one on 15th lasting 5½ hours.

Leading the attack would 25-year-old Sqn Ldr Nettleton of 44 Squadron, while 97's element was in the hands of Sqn Ldr 'Flap' Sherwood DFC.

Rumours of a 'special' were confirmed when the selected crews were informed on the 16th that the raid was planned for the next day. They were not told of the target until the briefing at 11:00 hours on the 17th.

Out on the dispersals each Lancaster was filled with maximum fuel (2,154 gallons/9,792 litres) and loaded with four 1,000lb (453kg) bombs fitted with delayed fuses.

At 15:30 Nettleton eased his heavily laden bomber, R5508, off Waddington's grass runway followed by the rest of his 'vic', flown by Fg Off John 'Ginger' Garwell DFM and Sgt George 'Dusty' Rhodes. Piloting the second trio were Flt Lt R R 'Nick' Sandford DFC, W/O Hubert Crum DFM and W/O John Beckett DFM.

The six set course for Selsey Bill before heading over the English Channel at less than 50ft (15m) to avoid German radar. The 97 Squadron formation had left Woodhall Spa at the same time.

Although the Lancasters flew unescorted, a large number of fighters and light bombers were making diversionary sweeps over northern France to draw off Luftwaffe fighters, and by the time they crossed the French coast the two squadrons had separated somewhat but hugged the contours of the Normandy countryside without incident.

109s ELEVEN O'CLOCK HIGH!

About 25 miles northwest of Evreux the Lancasters approached the village of Beaumont-le-Roger soon after 17:00. Just outside the village was the base of the headquarters flight and II Gruppe of Jagdgeschwader 2 'Richthofen'. The Messerschmitt 109F-4s of JG 2 had been scrambled to engage the diversionary sweeps.

By the greatest of ill luck 44's formation flew past the airfield just as the fighters were returning, JG 2's war diary vividly describing the coincidence: "But then – what's going on across the far side of the field? Incredible, British four-engined bombers! Three – no, six of them! Slowly they roar past low overhead, looking for all the world like a shoal of clumsy carp.

"Our fighters are still landing. Haven't any of them seen the enemy bombers? Yes, there – one has spotted them just as he is about to touch down. He guns his engine, retracts his undercarriage and chases off after them. Other fighters follow, some that have already landed quickly take off again. They hurl themselves upon the bombers."

From *V-for-Vic*, Beckett broke radio silence: "109s, eleven o'clock high!" The bombers closed up to give mutual support as they saw the fighters overshoot the airfield and turn towards them. Hauptmann Karl-Heinz Greisert closed and sent a hail of fire into Beckett's aircraft ➲

ABOVE
Nettleton's Lancaster casting a shadow while practising low flying before the attack.

ABOVE RIGHT
Messerschmitt Bf 109Fs of JG 2 at Beaumont-le-Roger, April 1941.
VIA JOHN WEAL

BOTTOM RIGHT
The shattered remains of a Lancaster, a grim testament to the brief fight over Beaumont-le-Roger.

which ploughed into the ground and exploded.

Feldwebel Alexander Bleymuller attacked Crum's *T-for-Tare*, sending shards of Perspex around the cockpit. Crum was injured but grimly held position as his aircraft took further hits which wounded Sgt John Miller in the mid-upper turret and set the port wing on fire. Ordering the bomb load to be jettisoned, Crum fought for control and managed to force-land in a wheat field.

Unteroffizier Otto Pohl engaged Sandford's *P-for-Peter*. Despite desperate evasion, including reportedly flying *under* power lines, with engines ablaze R5506's wingtip caught the ground and cartwheeled to destruction. It was Pohl's first victory and JG's thousandth.

The Bf 109s turned their attention to Nettleton's trio, which continued grimly on in close formation. Leading the chase was JG 2's Kommodore, Major Walter Oesau, with wingman Oberfeldwebel Fritz Edelmann. The pair chased *H-for-Harry*, skippered by Rhodes, and although Edelmann was wounded by return fire Oesau closed to about 30ft behind before

opening a devastating burst of fire. The Lancaster's port engines and starboard wing erupted in flames before the stricken bomber reared up to the vertical and crashed. It was Oesau's 101st victory.

In four minutes, two-thirds of the 44 Squadron formation had gone and Nettleton's and Garwood's two surviving aircraft had been damaged.

TARGET IN SIGHT

Short of fuel the Messerschmitts withdrew and, with Garwell's *A-for-Able* tucked in close, Nettleton pressed on for the target, still several hundred miles away. The 97 Squadron formation, which had not encountered the Bf 109s, and Nettleton and Garwell ploughed on, enduring occasional bursts of flak as the enemy was now fully alerted.

Ten miles south of the target the 44 Squadron pair turned on their final

"IN FOUR MINUTES, TWO-THIRDS OF THE 44 SQUADRON FORMATION HAD GONE AND NETTLETON'S AND GARWOOD'S SURVIVING AIRCRAFT HAD BEEN DAMAGED."

run in clear weather and excellent visibility – and, as they crested a ridge, saw Augsburg before them. Immediately a barrage of flak opened up. The aiming point was a T-shaped shed within the factory complex and it was sighted, looking exactly like the models they had seen at the earlier briefing.

With rooftops flashing beneath them, the Lancasters ran in, line astern. Once the 'bombs gone' call had been made, Nettleton swung west, his crew having the satisfaction of seeing whole sections of the shed and surrounding buildings erupt.

Having gallantly stuck with his leader throughout, Garwell dropped his bombs. Flak then hit his Lancaster and the rear fuselage caught fire, R5510 crash-landing in fields near the town.

As Nettleton headed west into the setting sun, Sherwood's 97 Squadron

AUGSBURG RAID APRIL 17, 1942 THE TOLL

SKIPPER	AIRCRAFT	UNIT	CIRCUMSTANCE
Rhodes	L7536 'KM-H'	44 Sqn	Shot own by Bf 109s – 7 killed
Crum	L7548 'KM-T'	44 Sqn	Shot own by Bf 109s – 7 PoW
Beckett	L7565 'KM-V'	44 Sqn	Shot own by Bf 109s – 7 killed
Sandford	R5506 'KM-P'	44 Sqn	Shot own by Bf 109s – 7 killed
Garwell	R5510 'KM-A'	44 Sqn	Hit by flak 3 killed, 4 PoW
Sherwood	L7573 'OF-K'	97 Sqn	Hit by flak – 6 killed, 1 PoW
Mycock	R5513 'OF-P'	97 Sqn	Hit by flak – 7 killed

LEFT
The mass grave of most of Flt Lt Sandford's and W/O John Beckett's crews, of erected by the French at the communal cemetery at Beaumont-le-Roger.

formation planted bombs into the factory. His aircraft was shot down close to the target, while *P-for-Pip*, captained by W/O T Mycock DFC, blew up just after bombing. Badly damaged, the surviving four 97 Squadron Lancasters headed for home.

HIGH-RISK, HIGH PRICE

After a long, but uneventful, flight home, Nettleton's exhausted crew landed R5508 at Squires Gate, Blackpool, shortly before 01:00 on April 18. Seven aircraft and 49 aircrew were posted missing – see the panel.

For his courage and inspirational leadership Sqn Ldr John Nettleton was awarded the Victoria Cross. Every member of his crew was also decorated in what had been the most daring raid by Bomber Command of the war to date.

It had always been a high-risk operation, pressed home in the face of much opposition, and drew praise from all corners, including Winston Churchill, who wrote that they had "struck a vital point with deadly precision. We must plainly regard the attack as an outstanding achievement."

ABOVE
The Nettleton crew. Standing, left to right: Sgt Les Mutter DFM, F/Sgt Frank Harrison DFM, Flt Lt Charles McClure DFC, Sgt Don Huntley DFM. Seated, left to right: Plt Off Pat Dorehill DFC, Sqn Ldr John Nettleton VC, Plt Off Des Sands DFC, F/Sgt Charles Churchill DFM.

With thanks to the President of the Mess Committee at RAF Waddington for permission to use the image of the painting of the raid that hangs in the Officers' Mess. Also to John Weal for access to the JG 2 diary and images. All images RAF Waddington archive unless noted. ●

ABOVE
A reconnaissance photo taken a few days after the raid, showing the extent of the damage to the diesel works.

GEORGE

PATRICK OTTER PROFILES THE AUSTRALIAN WAR MEMORIAL'S
W4783, THE "LANC THAT'LL ALWAYS GET YOU HOME"

George's story began with the formation of 460 Squadron Royal Australian Air Force at Molesworth, then in Northamptonshire, in November 1941. Soon afterwards the unit moved to the new airfield at Breighton, just east of Selby, on January 4, 1942. Equipped with Wellington IVs, 460 was led by the tough Wg Cdr Keith Kaufmann, one of six Australian brothers serving in the armed forces.

The Yorkshire home was always going to be a temporary one for 460. New airfields were being built in north Lincolnshire for 1 Group, but 460 was destined for something a little better than the Nissen-hutted, prefabricated hangar-equipped bases being built for some of its neighbours.

Under a deal struck with the Australian Government, RAAF bomber squadrons were to get the best airfields where possible: Leconfield, Waddington and, in 460's case, Binbrook – all pre-war 'Expansion' era with substantial buildings and facilities.

With the Wellingtons, 460 had gone through a baptism of fire; losing 29 on operations between March and the end of September 1942. This was a loss rate of 5.4%, the highest in Bomber Command. It must have come as some relief when crews heard they were to switch to 'heavies'.

The initial plan was for 1 Group to fly Halifax IIs. A conversion unit was set up at Holme-on-Spalding Moor, Yorkshire, for 460 and its neighbours, 101 Squadron, while south of the Humber 103 Squadron had its own conversion flight and began operations with the Handley Page bomber in August 1942. However, the successful introduction of Lancasters in 5 Group and the problems being encountered in 4 Group with the Halifax led to a change of policy: 1 Group was to get Lancasters.

AUSTRALIAN DEBUT

On October 20, 1942, 460 Squadron was notified it would be re-equipped with Lancasters and two days later the first batch of Mk.Is arrived from Woodford. Among them was

W4783, built by Metropolitan-Vickers at Trafford Park, Manchester. To go with its new squadron code of 'AR', W4783 was allocated the individual letter 'G'. (Originally 460 had flown with the code letters 'UV'.) So was born *G-for-George*.

The unit's debut with the new type occurred on the night of December 6/7 with a raid on Mannheim, Germany, *George* being one of ten which left Breighton, all returning safely. Flown on that sortie by F/Sgt Alec Saint-Smith and crew, who went on to complete their tour with a further 12 operations on W4783.

Over the coming months *George* flew regularly as 460's two flights contributed to most of the heavy raids on German, French and Italian targets, largely in the hands of NCO crews. The one exception was on the

⟶

BELOW
'George' amid the emotive display at the Australian War Memorial.
KEY-DUNCAN CUBITT

ABOVE
A well-worn 'George'
at Binbrook in June
1943, not long after
460 Squadron arrived
from Breighton. The
bomb tally shows 42
operations, the 42nd
being to Mulheim on
the night of June 22/23.
Left to right: Sqn Ldr
Eric Camplin DFC, W/O
Jack Panos, W/O Derek
Scruton, F/Sgt Max
Burcher, F/Sgt Charles
Crook and F/Sgt George
Petersen. Camplin is
not recorded as having
flown 'George' in action
but went on to complete
his second tour with
460, earning a DSO.
AUTHOR'S COLLECTION

ABOVE RIGHT
'George' at Binbrook
with an unidentified
crew after completing
its 90th 'op'.
AUTHOR'S COLLECTION

iconic raids of the war, the attack on the rocket experimental site at Peenemünde. *George* was among 324 Lancasters, 218 Halifaxes and 54 Stirlings sent to destroy the site on the Baltic coast.

The attack was carried out in full moonlight and Bomber Command lost 40 aircraft, mostly in the second wave by which time German fighters, newly equipped with upward-firing cannon, had arrived. The 24 sent from Binbrook were in the first wave and all returned safely.

'BIG CITY'

Peenemünde marked *George's* 46th 'op' and the squadron's sign writers were having a hard time keeping up with the ever-increasing number of bomb tallies painted on the nose. The 48th was to Berlin, the first of 11 trips it

night of March 11, 1943 when 460's new CO, Wg Cdr Chad Martin, took W4783 to Stuttgart.

George was in the thick of the action during the four months of the Battle of the Ruhr, March to July 1943, often returning to Breighton with flak damage. On one occasion when it came back on three engines it had been holed in 17 places, on both wings, tailplane, fuselage, mid-upper turret, two propellers and undercarriage.

The last operational flight from Breighton for *George* was on May 4 when Fg Off J Henderson and crew were part of a force of 19 Lancasters from 460 involved in a raid on Dortmund, one failing to return. Shortly after returning, the unit was stood down ready to move south to Binbrook. This was accomplished in spectacular style, most of the ground staff being flown across the Humber into Lincolnshire in Horsa assault gliders.

HOME ON THE WOLDS

The squadron made Binbrook, in Lincolnshire's Wolds, its home for the remainder of the war. Today, a memorial stands in the nearby village to an outstanding squadron, one which went on to record the most Lancaster sorties both in 1 Group and the whole of Bomber Command.

It also dropped the highest tonnage of bombs of any Lancaster squadron – around 24,000 tons. In the process it lost 169 in action with a further 31 destroyed in crashes.

From those statistics, it is obvious that *George* was fortunate to survive. It was ironic that W4783 was

"CARTER AND CREW WERE LUCKY TO SURVIVE A RAID TO MÖNCHENGLADBACH WHEN THE BOMBER WAS HIT BY A 'SHOWER' OF INCENDIARIES, WRECKING MUCH OF THE TAIL AND GIVING THE REAR GUNNER THE FRIGHT OF HIS LIFE."

almost written off after a bizarre ground accident at Binbrook on the afternoon of July 3, 1943 when another Lancaster, DV172, caught fire. While being prepared for an attack on Cologne, incendiaries fell from DV172's bomb bay and ignited, exploding entire warload.

A second Lancaster, the veteran R5745, which had started its life with 207 Squadron at Waddington, also caught fire and blew up, the resulting blast badly damaging *George* on a nearby dispersal. Despite this destruction, 460 provided 17 aircraft for the raid that night.

Another six weeks passed before W4783 was operational again, just in time to take part in one of the

made to the 'Big City'.

F/Sgt Harry 'Cherry' Carter was at the controls that night for the first of 21 operations he and his crew flew in *George,* seven of them to Berlin.

Carter and crew were lucky to survive a raid to Mönchengladbach when the bomber was hit by a 'shower' of incendiaries, wrecking much of the tail and giving the rear gunner the fright of his life.

Another of *George's* Berlin trips was on the night of December 2/3 when 460 lost five of the 25 Lancasters sent to Berlin. Carter and his crew finished their tour in W4783 on Christmas Eve, one of the very few 460 crews to make it to 30 operations at this stage of the war.

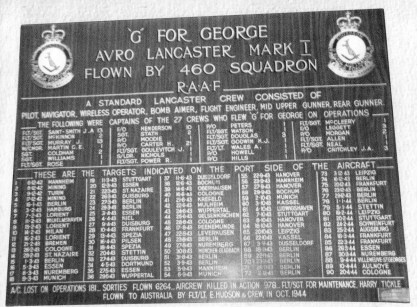

Initially, *George* was regarded as just another Lancaster by crews at Binbrook, albeit a veteran one. But as the list of bomb tallies increased, its reputation as the "Lanc that'll always get you home" began to grow. All the bomb symbols were painted free-hand by LAC Harry Lacey from Queensland.

Apart from the tallies, the colours of a DFM and a CGM ribbons, indicative of how aircrew at Binbrook regarded the aircraft, were applied. The early symbols included a tiny haloed figure denoting the 'ops' flown by Saint-Smith while another included a tiny Russian flag, recording a trip flown by F/Sgt Jack Murray who was noted for saying "All for Joe" whenever bombs were dropped on Germany.

Carter's trips were marked by a tiny pair of cherries, from his nickname, atop the bomb symbol.

Two weeks later Bomber Command's 'Black Thursday', December 16, *George* was attacked by a night-fighter over Berlin and was again damaged. Harry Carter, by now a warrant officer, managed to bring the damaged aircraft back to Binbrook, landing safely despite the foggy conditions which claimed many Lancasters and so many lives in 1 Group that night.

UNIDEXTER GUNNER

During its time with the squadron 29 different crews flew *George*, some, numerous times, others just once. One of the latter was a true 460 character,

F/Sgt Jan Goulevitch who could often be seen at Binbrook wearing a funeral director's top hat. He claimed to have 'found' it in a pub at nearby Laceby and adopted it as his own good luck charm.

Among the men Goulevitch flew with during his time at Binbrook was Plt Off Bob Dunstan, 460's legendary one-legged rear gunner. He had had a leg amputated while serving with the Australian Army as a machine gunner in North Africa. He returned to his home country but re-enlisted, joining the RAAF, and flew a tour with 460 as a rear gunner. The cramped conditions in a Lancaster rear turret meant that he not only had to leave his parachute in the fuselage, but his artificial leg as well.

Dunstan won a deserved DSO with 460 and went on to a successful political career in Australia. His path and that of *George* crossed once again when both had left Binbrook.

George's last trip to Berlin came on New Year's Day 1944, the aircraft's 78th operation. Soon it became evident that the aircraft was nearly past its best.

George was one of the 795 'heavies' sent to Nuremberg on the night of March 30/31, its 87th sortie. The crew noticed a dreadful vibration running through the airframe. It was so bad the navigator's instruments kept being shaken off his table and onto the floor.

Vibration or not, W4783 made it through the horrors of that night. F/Sgt Vic Neal and crew safely returned to Binbrook, unlike three others from 460 and 93 Lancasters ➲

BINBROOK BASE

Australian airmen at Binbrook soon after 460 Squadron moved from Breighton, mid-1943. The Lancaster in the background is W4988 'Q-for-Queenie', which crashed off the Swedish coast after being badly damaged by flak and fighters during a raid on Berlin in September 1943. The navigator was killed while three of the crew became prisoners and three others were interned in Sweden. 'Queenie' was among the first Lancasters delivered to the unit along with 'George' in the autumn of 1942. AUTHOR'S COLLECTION

"BINBROOK'S LEGENDARY STATION COMMANDER, GP CAPT HUGHIE EDWARDS, OFFICIALLY HANDED OVER 'GEORGE' TO THE AUSTRALIAN PEOPLE."

ABOVE RIGHT
AVM H N Wrigley,
AOC RAAF Overseas
HQ, shaking the
hand of Flt Sgt
Harry Tickle before
boarding 'George' at
Adelaide, 1944.
KEY COLLECTION

and Halifaxes from other Bomber Command squadrons.

Two of *George's* final three operations from Binbrook were against the new 'transport' targets, Villeneuve-Saint-Georges and Aulnoye-Aymeries in France, both choke points for road and rail to help paralyse the movement of the German Army in the run-up to the invasion.

The 90th and final trip, to Cologne, took place on the night of April 20/21. Those last three operations were all with the crew of Fg Off John Critchley. As was evident that the end was near for the veteran Lancaster and after the 90th bomb tally, a DSO was added.

PRIME MINISTER'S GIFT

It was decided to retire W4783 and this coincided with a visit to Binbrook by the then Prime Minister of Australia, John Curtin, as part of his tour of Australian forces in this country. Binbrook's legendary station commander, Gp Capt Hughie Edwards VC, officially handed over *George* to the Australian people. The weary warrior was destined to be flown half way round the world.

During its time at both Breighton and Binbrook *George* had been under the care of F/Sgt Harry Tickle and his ground crew. Tickle had been with 460 since its inception and he was proud of never having lost a single Wellington or Lancaster under his charge. He had supervised numerous repairs, modifications and at least 12 engine changes on *George* and he was given the task of ensuring the

squadron's grand old lady was up to a final 12,000-mile journey.

The aircraft went to the Avro facility at Bracebridge Heath, Lincoln for a full overhaul, including another four new Merlins. Back at Binbrook, *George* was prepared for its epic journey. It wouldn't be the first Lancaster to be sent on a long flight. Two years earlier a Lancaster fresh off the production line was sent on a promotional tour to Canada and it was later used to serve as a pattern for Canadian Lancaster construction.

Another, ED930 *Q-for-Queenie*, was sent to Australia and New Zealand – see the feature *75 Lancs* which starts on page 28. *George* was intended to replace *Queenie* as a workhorse for the War Savings drive in Australia.

TROUBLE-FREE

George left Binbrook for Prestwick in Scotland with a tour-expired crew of six: Flt Lt Eddie Hudson DFC*, pilot; Fg Off Francis Smith DFC, flight engineer; Fg Off Wilf Gordon DFC, navigator; Fg Off Tom McCarthy DFC* bomb aimer; Fg Off Clive Tindale DFM, wireless operator; and Fg Off George Young DFM, gunner. Also on board were the indomitable Harry Tickle and technician Sgt Keith Ower.

They flew out of Prestwick on October 11, 1944, via Montreal, San Francisco, Hawaii, Fiji and New Caledonia before finally landing at RAAF Amberley, near Brisbane, on November 8 after a trouble-free flight. Two days later *George* was airborne again, heading for Rockhampton, Queensland where the pilot's father

was among the welcoming party to meet the aircraft.

Given the RAAF serial A66-2 (Queenie had been A66-1) George began a lengthy tour of Australia on which it was joined by men who had served with 460 at Binbrook. Among them was Bob Dunstan who had, rightly, become something of a celebrity in his own right in his native country.

In July 1945 *George* became surplus to requirements and, although it had long been the intention to preserve the Lancaster as part of an Australian war museum, it spent the next ten years tethered to the ground in a remote corner of Fairburn airfield in Canberra. During this time its camouflage paint peeled away, its 90 bomb symbols faded in the fierce sunlight and, sadly, it was also vandalised.

In 1955 the trustees of the Australian War Memorial in Canberra stepped in and decided *George* would form part of a new aeroplane hall at the museum. The building itself had never been designed to take something as big as a Lancaster and a number of World War One aircraft had to be moved out to accommodate the bomber.

A programme of restoration got under way, returning to its wartime status in 1977. Three years later the 460 Squadron Association presented a replica 4,000lb 'Cookie' bomb to display with the Lancaster. *George* is now the centrepiece of an incredible display, a worthy home for a loyal warrior that had brought its crew home safely 90 times. ●

INSPIRATION

WHEN AIRFIX LAUNCHED A MODEL LANCASTER, 'G-FOR-GEORGE' WAS THE SUBJECT. PATRICK OTTER REMEMBERS A KIT THAT HELPED CREATE UNTOLD DEVOTEES FOR AVRO'S BOMBER

Generations of boys and many adults as well, were inspired by a certain Lancaster. How many enthusiasts today can trace their affection for Avro's masterpiece back to long evenings spent with newspaper spread out on the dining table and the smell of glue in the air?

Airfix launched its 1:72-scale Lancaster I in 1958 and chose W4783 *G-for-George*. It went on to sell up to four million sets, one of the most successful model kits in history. According to Airfix's honorary archivist and secretary of the Airfix Collectors' Club, Jeremy Brook, *George* was selected in 1957 because it was a preserved airframe.

It was a major investment: moulds for the smaller aircraft then sold by Airfix cost an average of £2,000 a time but that for the Lancaster, complete with rotating turrets, came in at £7,686 – that's £192,150 in present-day values. The kit remained in production until 1980 in its original form before being replaced by a new version and further updated in 2013.

It wasn't until the mid-1960s that the Lancaster was sold in the famous box illustrated by artist Roy Cross showing *George* landing with its port outer on fire and wing, flaps and propeller all showing battle damage. While a second set of markings were included, for a 100 Squadron Lancaster, it was the 460 Squadron option that everyone was making.

The painting itself was so loved by modellers that it was re-released in 2005 with digital artwork by Adam Tooby, in homage to the Roy Cross painting.

FAMILY PROJECT

My son was around nine years old when we bought our kit, together with a set of Humbrol paints, a brush and glue. The instructions were good and assembly wasn't all that difficult, although those gun turrets could prove tricky. The painting was fairly straight forward: there were just three colours needed, earth brown, dark green and matt black.

The final job was always to fix the decals, or transfers. They needed a good soak in a saucer of warm water before they could be gently eased clear of the backing paper and then, very carefully, put in position.

Perfectionists would perhaps have given the completed model a coat of matt varnish and added the distinctive exhaust stains on the upper wings. But in our case an excited nine-year-old wanted *George* on display as soon as possible.

George survived for a couple of years or so before being badly damaged during an enthusiastic dusting operation. It was finally written off after a crash from a bedroom shelf. The model may have gone, but the enthusiasm for Lancasters remains.

With many thanks to Jeremy Brook, secretary of the Airfix Collectors' Club and honorary Airfix archivist at Hornby. ●

BELOW LEFT
Roy Cross, the artist whose original artwork on the Airfix kit box helped make it such a success.

BELOW
The striking original box cover of the Airfix 1:72 scale Lancaster depicting 'G-for-George'.

75 'LAN

TO CELEBRATE THE ANNIVERSARY OF THE LANCASTER GOING INTO COMBAT, JOSH LYMAN PROFILES THE LIFE AND TIMES OF 75 OF THE 7,000-PLUS BUILT, INCLUDING THE SURVIVORS

L7527

Built at Chadderton, the first production Lancaster, L7527, was test-flown at Woodford on October 31, 1941 by Sam Brown. It was used for trials by Avro and the Aeroplane and Armament Experimental Establishment at Boscombe Down.

It was next issued to 1654 Heavy Conversion Unit at Wigsley and used to hone crews ready for their first operational squadron. An accident in May 1943 put it out of action and after repair it was stored at 20 Maintenance Unit, Aston Down.

On March 3, 1944 L7527 went to war, albeit briefly, when it joined 15 Squadron as 'LS-A' at Mildenhall. Essen in Germany was the target for *A-for-Able*, skippered by Plt Off T Marsh, 23 days after L7527 joined the unit. The Lancaster is believed to have exploded near Aachen; all seven crew perished.

With much of its time spent in development flying, L7257 had a much longer life than most Lancasters, clocking just over 353 hours.

L7542

Delivered from Woodford in January 1942, L7542 joined 44 Squadron at Waddington. During an afternoon training sortie on February 7, it was in the circuit at nearby Skellingthorpe. On approach, the pilot got the wind direction wrong and made an abrupt manoeuvre to correct his error, only to lose control. The bomber hit a snowdrift and slithered to a halt, minus its undercarriage. Nobody was hurt, but Bomber Command had suffered its first Lancaster loss. Including test-flying for signing off at Woodford, L7542 had a flying life of just six hours.

Thirteen days later another Lancaster of 44 Squadron, L7538, lay on its belly, minus its undercarriage having been written off. It was one of the three delivered to 44 Squadron at Waddington on Christmas Eve, 1941 – see the *Debut* on page 18.

Wearing the codes 'KM-B', L7538 was too fast on finals and over-ran the runway at Waddington on February 20, 1942. Like the previous incident, the only injury was to the pilot's pride.

L7570

The second unit equipped with Lancasters was 97 Squadron at Coningsby, in January 1942. It was moved to nearby Woodhall Spa to begin operations on March 2. Lancaster I L7570 was among the first to be taken on, adopting the codes 'OF-B'.

On March 20 Fg Off E Rodley eased *B-for-Baker* off Woodhall Spa's runway, bound for the waters off the Frisian Islands on the northwest German coast where 97 was due to

CS'

achieve. It may have only got 17 miles (27km) from base, but this was combat flight and therefore Bomber Command's first operational Lancaster loss.

R5489

At a ceremony to inaugurate the massive factory established by Avro at Yeadon – the present-day Leeds-Bradford Airport – on March 26, 1942, the opportunity was taken to maximise publicity for the RAF's latest bomber by having two examples named by the guests of honour. Mk.Is R5489 and R5548 were unveiled as *George* and *Elizabeth* by King George VI and Queen Elizabeth. Yeadon was some way off completing its first Lancasters and

was well with the crew. The pilot had done a good job and, ordinarily, L7570 would have been recovered but the North Sea ended that idea and it was swamped by the incoming tide.

Lancaster *Baker* had mines in its bomb bay and a target to

carry out a mine-laying operation, code-named 'Gardening'. The take-off went wrong, the Lancaster's wing impacting the roof of a house on the airfield perimeter and L7570 limped southeast.

Rodley gave up all hopes of a recovery beyond the town of Boston, setting the Lancaster down on the shore near Freiston. One of the gunners was injured but otherwise all

both R5489 and R5548 had made the hop over the Pennines from Woodford for the event.

George and *Elizabeth* joined 44 and 97 Squadrons, respectively becoming 'KM-X' and 'OF-A'; neither saw the year out. While training, R5489 encountered difficulties on approach to Waddington on August 16 and crashed near Branston; killing two of the crew and badly injuring another. At dispersal at Woodhall Spa on December 28, a photo-flash munition exploded in R5548's bomb bay and it was destroyed by fire; there were no casualties.

"TUCKED INSIDE ONE OF THE DISPLAY HALLS IS AN EXHIBIT THAT IS OFTEN OVERLOOKED BY VISITORS, YET IT IS ONE OF THE COLLECTION'S MANY JEWELS. BEFORE JOINING THE MUSEUM IN MARCH 1974, THE SMALL FUSELAGE SECTION OF LANCASTER I W4964 SERVED AS A GARDEN SHED!"

ABOVE
In the later months of 2016, the interior of W4964 was turned into the 'Weeping Lancaster' commemoration at the Newark Air Museum.

ABOVE RIGHT
Veteran of 106 'ops', part of the fuselage of Mk.I W4964 'Johnnie Walker – Still Going Strong' is an impressive exhibit at the Newark Air Museum. BOTH HOWARD HEELEY

R5493

It was late March 1942 when the tragic abbreviation FTR – failed to return – appeared against Lancaster I R5493's records. Delivered from Woodford, it joined 44 Squadron and was painted up as 'KM-M'. As related in *Debut* on page, it departed Waddington on the evening of March 24 en route to the coast of Lorient, France, on a 'Gardening' sortie. Probably the victim of flak, *M-for-Mother* was noted as FTR the following morning.

F/Sgt Lyster Warren-Smith and his crew of seven – including a 'second-dickie' pilot – were never recovered and all are commemorated on the walls at the Air Forces Memorial, Runnymede, Surrey. (A second-dickie was a pilot, shortly to captain his own aircraft, gaining operational experience with 'old hands'.)

R5508

The feature *Debut* on page 18 deals with the daring, and exceptionally unlucky, daylight raid by the Lancasters of 44 and 97 Squadrons against a factory making submarine diesel engines at Augsburg, Germany, on April 17, 1942. Of the 44 Squadron machines, only Sqn Ldr John Nettleton's R5508 'KM-B' returned. Nettleton was awarded the Victoria Cross on the 28th.

Leading a raid from Dunholme Lodge on July 12, 1943 Wg Cdr Nettleton VC of 44 Squadron was captaining Mk.I ED331 'KM-Z' on

the long run to Turin, Italy. On the return leg, his Lancaster is thought to have been engaged by a night-fighter near the French coast and all eight on board died.

Lancaster R5508 was at least the second *B-for-Baker* with 44 Squadron – see L7538 above. It was retired from frontline service at Waddington in October 1942 and moved to 1660 Heavy Conversion Unit at Swinderby, taking on the codes 'TV-C'. After a period of storage at 38 Maintenance Unit at Llandow the veteran R5508 was returned to an operational unit.

Based at Mildenhall, 15 Squadron moved to Wyton in August 1946, and R5508 served from both bases, coded 'LS-C'. By the first weeks of 1947 the first Lincolns were arriving and on January 15, 1947, R5508, its historical significance probably long since forgotten, was struck off charge and scrapped.

R5561

Sir Arthur 'Bomber' Harris placed considerable faith in the idea of hitting German cities with a stream of a thousand bombers. The propaganda value, both at home and within the Reich, would be immense. Operation Millennium, the first 'Thousand Bomber Raid' singled out Cologne for the night of May 30/31, 1942. There were two other 'Thousand' operations, both in June, targeting Essen and Bremen.

For the May 30/31 raid, 1,047 aircraft were amassed, including a

force of 73 Lancasters. Only one of these failed to return: Plt Off J B Underwood's Mk.I R5561 of 61 Squadron, based at Syerston. The aircraft crashed to the northwest of its target, all seven on board were killed. Delivered to 61 Squadron 33 days previously, R5561 had a total of just 37 flying hours to its credit.

R5689

In September 1942, a series of photographs were released of 50 Squadron Mk.I R5689, which have been well used by newspapers, magazines and books ever since. The pilot for that sortie was Sqn Ldr Hugh Everitt and, going by some of the images, he and his crew had a great time during the 'shoot'. Everitt had a long career with the RAF; by the early 1960s he was flying Vickers Valiant V-bombers, retiring as Gp Capt G H Everitt DSO DFC* in 1967.

While Everitt had a long way to go with the RAF after the air-to-air session, R5689 did not see the month of September 1942 out. After testing at Woodford, it was delivered to 50 Squadron at Swinderby in June 1942, taking on the codes 'VN-N'. Skippered by Australian Sgt E J Morley, *N-for-Nuts* set off on a 'Gardening' – mine-laying – sortie on September 19, 1942. On return, over the village of Thurlby, just east of Swinderby, the port engines of the Lancaster went silent and the bomber crash landed. Canadian gunner Sgt J R Gibbons was

tragically killed, but the remainder of the crew all survived the incident.

R5868

Displayed in the Bomber Hall at the RAF Museum, Hendon, Lancaster I R5868 *S-for-Sugar* has a quote from Reichmarshall Hermann Goering painted on the nose. It reads as follows: "No enemy aircraft will fly over the Reich territory". Close by these words are 139 bomb tallies, which took about 795 hours of operational flying to achieve during which it dropped about 466 tons of bombs on the very land Goering had declared sacrosanct.

That number of 'ops' was only surpassed by one other Lancaster – ED888 'PM-M' of 103 Squadron – see page 35.

Take a look in the 'Research' section of the RAF Museum's exceptional website. There the public can download *32 pages* of the official

history of R5868. Hence the task of putting together a *brief* history of this incredible survivor is nigh on impossible and the first and last of those 139 'ops', and a close shave in November 1943, must suffice.

Built by Metropolitan-Vickers at Trafford Park, Manchester, R5868 was tested at Woodford in June 1942. Taken on charge by 83 Squadron at Scampton on June 29, 1942 it was given the code letters 'OL-Q'. Sqn Ldr Ray Hilton DFC, commander of 'B' Flight, eased R5868 off the runway at just gone midnight on July 9 with 1,260 four-pounder incendiaries in the bomb bay bound for Wilhelmshaven, Germany. Sixty-seven sorties later, on August 15, 1943, *Q-for-Queenie* completed its last 'run' with 83.

In September R5868 arrived at Bottesford, joining 467 Squadron Royal Australian Air Force, and was coded 'PO-S'. The stay at Bottesford

was not long and on November 11, R5868 was ferried to Waddington, 467's new base.

Sortie No.82 was to 'The Big City' – Berlin – with Fg Off Jack Colpus at the helm on November 26, 1943. Just after bomb release, *S-for-Sugar* was coned by searchlights and Colpus corkscrewed and dived to throw the enemy off the scent. At 20,000ft or so, the rear gunner reported that they had collided with another aircraft. After much agonising, and not knowing the full extent of the damage, Jack put Sugar down at Linton-on-Ouse, Yorkshire, with 5ft missing from the wing tip.

(The other aircraft turned out to be Lancaster I DV311 *P-for-Peter* of Skellingthorpe-based 61 Squadron. Its crew also lived to tell the tale.)

Sugar's 139th and last 'op' was on April 23, 1945 when Fg Off Laurie Baker took it to Flensburg in Germany, but he did not drop ➲

ABOVE
Hercules-engined Mk.II DS704 of 408 Squadron RCAF.

BELOW
Lancaster II DS723 'B-for-Baker' of 408 Squadron RCAF.

his eight thousand-pounders and half-dozen 500-pounders because of the 10/10ths cloud cover over the harbour. Six days later Italian partisans killed Mussolini and 48 hours after that Hitler shot himself; the war in Europe was over bar the formalities.

The venerable Lancaster was issued to 15 Maintenance Unit at Wroughton, on August 23, 1945. For a decade from 1960, R5868 became a well-known landmark 'guarding' the main entrance at Scampton. In March 1972, it was installed at Hendon in the markings of 467 Squadron.

W4774

Within the French town of Le Creusot, to the west of Geneva, was the massive Schneider armaments plant. It was a priority target for Bomber Command, but extensive housing estates close by meant a precision strike was desirable and in October 1942 that meant by daylight and at low-level. The commanding officer of Scampton-based 49 Squadron, Wg Cdr Leonard Slee DSO DFC led a force of 94 Lancasters.

Six were detailed to hit the power station at Montchanin, to the southeast of the main factory. Among these was Mk.I W4774 built by Metropolitan-Vickers, captained by Sqn Ldr W D Corr DFC of 61 Squadron at Syerston. Corr's aircraft attacked at such low level that it collided with buildings and crashed. Gunner Sgt R Turtle survived to become a prisoner of war; all the rest of the crew were killed. It was the only Lancaster of the entire raid that failed to return.

W4783

Built by Metropolitan-Vickers at Trafford Park, Mk.I W4783 is one of 17 Lancasters to survive intact. Dramatically displayed at the Australian War Memorial in Canberra, W4783 was issued to 460 Squadron Royal Australian Air Force at Breighton on October 22, 1942. It took on the codes 'AR-G' and its story is detailed in the feature *George*, on page 22.

W4964

A couple of miles northeast of Newark-on-Trent is the former Winthorpe airfield, now largely occupied by the town's showground. From early 1943 to the summer of 1945, Winthorpe was the home of 1661 Heavy Conversion Unit which, among other types, operated all the RAF's four-engined bombers, the Halifax, Lancaster and Stirling.

Also at Winthorpe and open since April 1973 is the Newark Air Museum. Tucked inside one of the display halls is an exhibit that is often overlooked by visitors, yet it is one of the collection's many jewels. Before joining the museum in March 1974, the small fuselage section of Lancaster I W4964 served

served in a Lincolnshire garden until its long-term future was assured by the museum.

BT308

All things being equal, the serial numbers for prototypes usually precede the production examples. This was not the case with the Lancaster, which was essentially a development of another type, already being churned out of the factories. Early Lancaster serial numbers were allocated long before and intended for the twin-engined Manchester.

The very first Lancaster was taken from Manchester jigs and created at the Avro Chadderton factory and throughout this process it was referred

LEFT
Highlight of the summer of 2014, Lancasters FM213 and PA474, a once-in-a-lifetime experience.
DARREN HARBAR

"TWO OF WILLIAM'S CREW WERE KILLED, MORRISON AND THREE OTHERS MANAGED TO EVADE, WHILE THE TAIL GUNNER BECAME A PRISONER OF WAR. IT IS BELIEVED THAT DS704 WAS THE VICTIM OF 'FRIENDLY FIRE'; SHOT DOWN BY THE TAIL GUNNER OF ANOTHER LANCASTER."

as a garden shed in Gainsborough!

Built by Metropolitan-Vickers in Manchester, it was issued to 9 Squadron at Bardney in the spring of 1943. It took on the codes 'WS-J' – still visible today – and the name *Johnnie Walker – Still Going Strong* was applied to the nose. This Lancaster went on to complete an incredible 106 operations. As described in *Bowling 'The Beast' Over* on page 66, its 'century' was against the warship *Tirpitz* in September 1944.

The following month *J-for-Johnnie* was retired and on December 9, 1944 it became instructional airframe 4922M. It was struck off charge in November 1949 and chopped up. An enterprising householder recognised the potential of an upper section of fuselage and, with wooden walls 'fore and aft' it

to as the Manchester III. As related in *Building a Legend* on page 14, Sam Brown and his deputy, Bill Thorn, took BT308 for its 40-minute maiden flight on January 9, 1941 from Ringway – now Manchester Airport. The second Lancaster prototype, DG595, was not far behind. Sam and Bill were at the controls at Ringway on May 13, 1941.

DS704

As related in *Building a Legend*, page 14, as an insurance against interruptions in the supply of Rolls-Royce Merlins, Avro developed the Mk.II powered by Bristol Hercules radials. The prototype, DT810, was first flown from Woodford by Sam Brown on November 26, 1941.

Production of the Mk.II was entrusted to Armstrong Whitworth Aircraft (AWA), the bulk of the

ABOVE
Delivered from Canada in June 1945, Mk.X FM142 never saw operational service.

LEFT
Stills from a well-known film showing drop trials of the 'bouncing bomb', probably with Vickers test pilot 'Mutt' Summers piloting.

200 manufactured being assembled at Sywell, which was used until the massive factory at Bitteswell was ready. The first example was DS601, which AWA test pilot Charles Turner-Hughes flew for the first time on August 12, 1942 from the grass at Sywell. Tests were a one-way affair, ending at the company's site at Baginton.

Lancaster II DS704 was first flown at Sywell on August 26, 1943.

It was issued to 408 Squadron Royal Canadian Air Force at Linton-on-Ouse before the month was out, becoming 'EQ-W'. On the night of December 20 *W-for-William*, skippered by Australian Plt Off L Morrison, was bound for Frankfurt. Over Belgium, DS704 was fired upon and the crew abandoned the bomber. Two of *William's* crew were killed, Morrison and three others managed to evade, while the tail gunner became a prisoner of war.

It is believed DS704 was the victim of 'friendly fire'; shot down by the tail gunner of another Lancaster. The Mk.II was one of 17 Lancasters lost that night.

ABOVE
Lancaster III JA847 'PG-C' of 619 Squadron, Woodhall Spa, December 1943. PETE WEST

LEFT
Mk.I HK541 was the aerodynamic test-bed for the 'Tiger Force' long-range 'saddle tank. modification.

LEFT
The one-off Lancaster 10-DC, KB851, with a Ryan Firebee drone under each wing.

BELOW
The first Victory Aircraft-built Lancaster X, KB700, at Woodford for assessment in September 1943. KEC

DS723

Built by Armstrong Whitworth as a Hercules-engined Mk.II, DS723 joined 408 Squadron Royal Canadian Air Force at Linton-on-Ouse in the autumn of 1943, becoming 'EQ-B'. Appointed commanding officer of 408 on October 28, Wg Cdr Alex Mair DFC was at the helm of DS723 as it took off from Linton at 17:11 hours on November 26. The destination was the 'Big City' – Berlin – and *B-for-Baker* dropped its bombs and turned for home. Nothing more was ever heard of the aircraft, or Mair and his six crew. It was one of two Lancasters lost by 408 that night, although the crew of DS712 did not suffer any fatalities.

DV372

Named *Old Fred*, from its individual squadron letter, *F-for-Freddie*, the cockpit section of DV372 is a well-known exhibit at the Imperial War Museum in London. Built by Metropolitan-Vickers as a Mk.I, DV372 was issued to 467 Squadron Royal Australian Air Force at Waddington in November 1943 taking on the codes 'PO-F'. Twelve months later it was training crews for operational service with 1651 Heavy Conversion Unit at Woolfox Lodge. Struck off charge in October 1945, the cockpit survived and joined the museum in 1960.

ED888

When a unit had a large complement, often a squadron with three flights totalling 30 aircraft, individual code letters would exceed those of the alphabet. What to do beyond *Z-for-Zebra*? Sometimes aircraft were given a letter with a small '2' after it, just like the mathematical 'squared' symbol.

Chadderton-built Mk.III ED888 served with 103 Squadron as 'PM-M²' and was referred to as 'Mike Squared' accordingly. It also received other nicknames, when it became the Lancaster with the largest ever number of operations to its credit – 'King of Lancasters' and 'Mother of Them All'.

Delivered from Woodford to Elsham Wolds in April 1943, ED888 joined 103 Squadron's 'B' Flight, becoming 'PM-M'. The first of ED888's 66 'ops' with 103 was to Dortmund, Germany, on May 4/5. On November 25, 1943 'C' Flight of 103 Squadron was hived off, becoming 576 Squadron; ED888 ➔

"FIVE DAYS AFTER KB700 WAS FIRST TESTED, IT WAS NAMED 'RUHR EXPRESS' WHEN A BOTTLE OF CHAMPAGNE, WITH PURPOSELY THIN GLASS SO AS NOT TO DAMAGE THE BOMBER'S SKIN, WAS BROKEN ACROSS THE NOSE."

was part of the transfer, taking up the code 'UL-V²'. The Lancaster clocked 65 operations with 576 and on October 31, 1944 it re-joined 103 Squadron. This involved no more than a change of dispersal parking and the painting of new code letters, that's when ED888 took up the famous 'PM-M²'.

An accident brought 'Mike Squared's' service with 103 Squadron to an end in February 1945, after 9 'ops'. This brought the Lancaster's tally to 140 – an achievement that was not beaten. Adding to this impressive effort, ED888's gunners had accounted for two Luftwaffe fighters. Repaired, ED888 was sent to 10 Maintenance Unit at Hullavington with 974 flying hours 'on the clock'. The 'King of Lancasters' was struck off charge on January 8, 1947 and scrapped. The Air Historic Branch had secured Mk.I R5868 – see page 31 – for museum purposes two years previously and it seems that ED888's significance was forgotten, or overlooked.

ED930

Plans to build Lancasters in Australia never came to fruition, although the Lincoln was produced by the Government Aircraft Factory at Melbourne, Victoria – see *Legacy*, on page 94.

Nevertheless Mk.III ED930 was delivered from Woodford to 39 Maintenance Unit at Colerne in preparation to be issued to the Royal Australian Air Force in May 1943.

Named *Queenie VI*, ED930 departed Prestwick on May 22, 1943 routing across the Atlantic, through Canada, the USA and the Pacific; arriving in Australia after 13 days. Its original role as a pattern aircraft had been superseded and instead it toured the continent encouraging recruitment and the purchase of war bonds.

In June 1943, the Lancaster carried out a brief tour of New Zealand. *Queenie* hit the headlines

on October 22 when it flew under Sydney Harbour Bridge. Four days later the Lancaster was out of the limelight when a landing accident at Evans Head, New South Wales, looked set to have it declared a write-off. With spares oceans away, and no combat role possible, *Queenie* should have been broken up. Instead, replacement parts were sourced in Canada and by April 1944 the Lancaster was back in the air.

By this time it was wearing the RAAF serial A66-1 and had forsaken its standard camouflage for overall natural metal with blue-and-white South East Asian Command roundels. With the arrival of the veteran Mk.I W4783 *George* in Australia in late 1944 – see page 22 – ED930 was side-lined and in October 1946 was downgraded to instructional airframe status. It was sold for scrap in June 1948.

ED932

The 22 Lancaster IIIs converted to carry the 'bouncing bomb' – code-named 'Upkeep' – designed by Barnes Wallis, were given the designation Avro Type 464 Provisioning. The term 'Provisioning' was designed to make a very special modification sound remarkably mundane. To emphasise the importance of these aircraft, they carried the suffix '/G' to their serial numbers; for example, Sqn Ldr H M 'Dinghy'

Young's *A-for-Able* was marked ED887/G.

At the end of a tour with 106 Squadron, Wg Cdr Guy Gibson DSO* DFC* was selected to head a unit at Scampton for special duties: 617 Squadron was formed on March 23, 1943. On April 30 'Provisioning' Mk.III ED932/G 'AJ-G' was issued to 617 and it was this machine that Gibson captained during Operation Chastise, the breaching of the Möhne and Eder dams on May 16/17.

After the raid, ED932/G was recoded as *V-for-Victor* and on February 7, 1945 it was retired to 46 Maintenance Unit, Lossiemouth. In August 1946, it was brought out of storage for use in Operation Guzzle, the disposal of the remaining stocks of Upkeep weapons in the North Sea. Dropping these by any aircraft not equipped with the special cradle in the bomb bay would have been very difficult. The Guzzle aircraft were nominally on charge with the Lincoln-equipped 61 Squadron at Hemswell but carried the codes of the Scampton Station Flight; ED932 becoming 'YF-C'.

On take-off at Scampton on November 8, 1946, while taking part in Guzzle, ED932 suffered an accident. Damage was assessed as Category Ac; repair was possible on site, but was beyond the means of resident units. The aircraft that led Bomber Command's most famous exploit, its captain being awarded a Victoria Cross, was declared struck off charge on July 29, 1947 and scrapped.

EE134

Lancaster III EE134 was delivered to Fiskerton in May 1943, joining 49 Squadron, becoming 'EA-B'. In September, it moved to Woodhall Spa to operate with 619 Squadron until November 1944. During this time 619 changed bases, in turn:

Coningsby, Dunholme Lodge and Strubby.

Carrying 619's codes 'PG-Y', EE134 chalked up 99 operations, which were tallied under the cockpit. Painted above them was a heraldic shield, quartered with four different symbols: boomerangs, the devil, a crab and a skull with two dice. The unit was never issued an official badge and this may have been an attempt to make up for the omission. The Latin motto Semper in Excretia, politely translates as 'Always in the Excrement'.

The veteran was taken off operations in November 1944 and issued to 5 Lancaster Finishing School at Syerston. It was coded 'CE-O', gaining a small O-for-Oboe under the nose turret, although the impressive bomb tallies and nose-art from its days

and was retired in September 1964.

Put on display at the National Exhibition Grounds in Toronto, Ontario, from 1964 to 1999 it was then acquired by the Toronto Aerospace Museum and moved to Downsview, Toronto.

FM136

Built at Malton, Canada, Mk.X FM136 was delivered to the UK in May 1945 and put into store at 32 Maintenance Unit, St Athan. Returned to Canada, it was taken on charge by the Royal Canadian Air Force on September 7, 1945. Converted to a Mk.10-MR maritime patroller, it served with 404 Squadron from Greenwood, Nova Scotia, and 407 Squadron at Comox, British Columbia, until it was paid off in April 1961.

Mk.X FM159. It is painted in the colours of Mk.III ND811 'F2-T' of 635 Squadron in which Sqn Ldr Ian Bazalgette earned a posthumous Victoria Cross on August 4, 1944. It was dedicated to Bazalgette's memory in 1990.

Arriving in Britain in May 1945, FM159 was placed in storage at 32 Maintenance Unit, St Athan before setting off back to Canada on August 30. After service with the Royal Canadian Air Force as a maritime patrol Mk.10-MR, it was struck off charge in October 1960 and prepared for scrapping at Calgary, Alberta. George White, Howie Armstrong and Fred Garratt of the Nanton Lancaster Society clubbed together and paid $513 for FM159, moving it to Nanton, in September 1960. The Lancaster

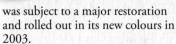

with 619 were retained. The Mk.III was struck off charge on March 31, 1945 and was snapped up by Rolls-Royce, moving the short distance west to the company's test airfield at Hucknall.

There EE134 was turned into a rigidly mounted test rig, eventually losing its outer engines and wings. Its first task was to test the Merlin 102s, cowlings and propellers for the Avro Tudor airliner, the prototype of which first flew in June 1945. Beyond that, the 99-op warrior tested other Merlins and was used for fire control experiments before it was scrapped.

FM104

As detailed in *Building a Legend* on page 14, Victory Aircraft at Malton, Ontario, Canada, built Lancaster Xs for Bomber Command. Mk.X FM104 was ferried across the Atlantic in May 1945 and was issued to 428 Squadron Royal Canadian Air Force (RCAF) at Middleton St George now Durham Tees Valley Airport. It was returned to Canada on June 10, 1945 and taken on charge by the RCAF that August. Eventually it was converted to Mk.10-MR maritime patrol status

Acquired by the Air Museum of Calgary, Alberta, it was allocated the civil registration CF-NJQ. From 1961 to 1990 it was displayed outside the Centennial Planetarium at Calgary. It joined the Aero Space Museum Calgary in 1990, now known as the Hangar Flight Museum with the superb catchline 'A Museum with Altitude'. Carrying the nose-art *Lady Orchid* to port, the starboard side has the name *Jenkins Express*, FM136 was dedicated to the memory of Fg Off Ronnie Jenkins in 2011.

FM142

Of the 130 Lancaster Xs built by Victory Aircraft in Canada with serials prefixed 'FM', a total of 71 were ferried to Britain, placed straight into store and never used. In the summer of 1947 all were struck off charge. Typical of these was FM142, which arrived in Britain in June 1945 and was sold for scrap on May 7, 1947.

FM159

The main exhibit at the Bomber Command Museum of Canada at Nanton, Alberta, is Victory-built

was subject to a major restoration and rolled out in its new colours in 2003.

FM212

Struck off charge by the Royal Canadian Air Force (RCAF) on October 9, 1964, Lancaster X FM212 was acquired by the People of Windsor and placed on display in the Ontario city's Jackson Park. Built at Malton, Ontario, it was never sent to the UK and was taken on charge by the RCAF in September 1946. It was converted to Mk.10-P guise and used extensively for photo-mapping. Acquired by the Canadian Historical Aircraft Association in 2005, FM212 is undergoing long-term restoration at Windsor Airport.

FM213

During the summer of 2014 the Canadian Warplane Heritage (CWH) Mk.X and the Battle of Britain Memorial Flight's Mk.I PA474 generated all sorts of emotions as the pair toured venues and events across the UK in a once-in-a-lifetime get-together. ➲

ABOVE LEFT
Mk.10-AR KB976 at Calgary on July 4, 1964 – the last flight of an RCAF Lancaster.
LARRY MILBURY
VIA ANDY THOMAS

ABOVE
Lancaster X G-BCOH during its ferry flight to the UK, May 1975.
VIA DICK RICHARDSON

RIGHT
Waltham-based Mk.III
ND458 'Abel Mabel'
of 100 Squadron,
1944. KEC

BELOW
The Boulton Paul-
modified gust
alleviation trials
Mk.III ME540 at
Pendeford, 1951.

Joyous cries were mixed with the quiet memories of veterans. Based at Hamilton, Ontario, the CWH Lancaster is the only one in which members of the public can go flying.

Known as 'Vera', from the bomber's 419 Squadron codes 'VR-A', FM213 was built by Victory Aircraft in July 1945 and was later converted to Mk.10-MR maritime patrol configuration for operation by the Royal Canadian Air Force (RCAF). It was flown by 405 Squadron from Greenwood, Nova Scotia, and 107 Rescue Unit at Torbay, Newfoundland.

Retired from RCAF service in late 1963, FM213 was struck off charge on June 30, 1964 and put on display at Goderich, Ontario. With help from the Sulley Foundation in 1977, it was acquired from the Royal Canadian Legion by the CWH. Eleven years passed before it was completely restored and it flew on September 24, 1988 at Hamilton with the civilian registration C-GVRA. Known as the 'Mynarski Memorial Lancaster', it flies in the colours of the machine in which Plt Off Andrew Mynarski VC served – see KB726, opposite.

HK541

With the war in Europe moving to its inevitable outcome, plans were in hand for Bomber Command to shift its attentions to the Pacific theatre to take part in long-range raids on the Japanese mainland from bases in the Okinawa island chain. By February 1945 this scheme was known as 'Tiger Force' and 12 RAF bomber squadrons supplemented the USAAF Boeing B-29 Superfortress wings.

To extend the Lancaster's range, Avro devised a 1,200 gallon (5,455-litre) 'saddle' tank behind the cockpit and two machines were converted to try this out. Built by Vickers-Armstrong at Castle Bromwich, Mk.I HK541 served with 115 Squadron from Witchford as 'KO-P' before moving to 3 Lancaster Finishing School at Feltwell, finishing up at 1651 Heavy Conversion Unit at Wratting Common. Early in 1945 HK541 became the aerodynamic prototype for the saddle tank, going to the Aeroplane and Armament Experimental Establishment at Boscombe Down, by March 1945.

Brand new Mk.I SW544, built by Metropolitan-Vickers was converted to full saddle-tank status at Woodford and was taken to Boscombe in April 1945 for testing. Later SW544 was ferried through to Mauripur in India for endurance trials with 1577 Flight.

The atomic bombs of early August 1945 brought Japan to surrender and the need for 'Tiger Force' no longer

existed. Both HK541 and SW544 were retired to 10 Maintenance Unit at Hullavington and were sold for scrap in January 1947 and November 1946, respectively

JA847

Lancaster III JA847 *C-for-Charlie* of 619 Squadron took off from Woodhall Spa at 16:43 hours on December 2, 1943, bound for the 'Big City', Berlin. The following morning, it and EE170 *N-for-Nun* were posted as missing; never to return. It had been a devastating night for Bomber Command, as well as the two 619 machines, 40 other Lancasters were lost, out of force of 425.

Charlie had been issued to 619 direct from Woodford and when it departed Woodhall that evening had just less than 300 flying hours to its credit. Canadian Fg Off J F Bowyer was the skipper and one of three crew to perish that night. The Lancaster came down in Tegel Forest, to the north of the German capital. Four of the crew survived; all becoming prisoners of war.

KB700

As explained in *Building a Legend* (page 14) the appropriately-named Victory Aircraft was

formed at Malton, Ontario, to build Lancaster Xs for use by Bomber Command. Test pilot Ernie Taylor took first Canadian example, KB700 into the air for its maiden flight on August 1, 1943. Oddly, the Lancaster batch KB700 to KB999 were the first down the production line, preceding the alphabetically earlier FM100 to FM229, which began to appear in April 1945.

Five days after KB700 was first tested, it was named *Ruhr Express* when a bottle of Champagne, with purposely thin glass so as not to damage the bomber's skin, was broken across the nose. The wife of the Canadian Minister of Air, Charles 'Chubby' Power, officiated. Celebrations over, Sqn Ldr R J Lane and crew started KB700, ostensibly taking it off to war. Instead KB700 was ferried to Dorval, Montreal, to finish off testing. *Ruhr Express* arrived at Woodford on September 15 and was put through rigorous evaluation by Avro, getting glowing reports for its quality of build.

On October 5 KB700 was delivered to 405 Squadron Royal Canadian Air Force (RCAF) at Linton-on-Ouse where it was coded 'LQ-Q'. Plt Off Harold Floren was the skipper for KB700's first operation, taking off on November 22 for Berlin, but it was soon back, having suffered an engine problem.

Ruhr Express later served from Middleton St George – now Durham Tees Valley Airport – with 419 Squadron as 'VR-Z'. On January 2, 1945 KB700 overshot on approach to Middleton and while trying to remedy the situation its captain hit a tractor. All the crew scrambled out, but KB700 was a write-off.

KB726

The Canadian Warplane Heritage Lancaster – see FM213 – wears the colours of 419 Squadron Royal Canadian Air Force Mk.X KB726, with the codes 'VR-A'. It honours Plt Off Andrew Mynarski, who was awarded the Commonwealth's highest award for gallantry, the Victoria Cross.

Winnipeg-born Mynarski was the mid-upper gunner of 419 Squadron Malton-built X KB726, tasked to attack Cambrai, France, on the night of June 12/13, 1944. Captained by Fg Off A de Breyne RCAF, *A-for-Able* took off from Middleton St George at 21:44 hours.

The Lancaster was attacked by a Junkers Ju 88, both port engines failed and a fire broke out in the rear fuselage. The skipper ordered the crew to bale out but Mynarski saw that the rear gunner was trapped. Without hesitating he went through the flames to reach his colleague. In doing so, his clothing and parachute caught fire, but all his efforts to free the gunner were in vain.

Before retreating, Mynarski turned to the trapped gunner, Fg Off G P Brophy, stood to attention in his burning clothing and saluted before jumping from KB726. His descent was seen by the French people who recovered him, but Mynarski died from his injuries and burns. The rear gunner had a miraculous escape when *Able* crashed, and testified to Mynarski's supreme gallantry.

KB822

Bomber Command's last fatalities during offensive operations over Europe occurred on April 25, 1945. A force of 482 bombers was despatched in mid-afternoon to put the coastal artillery at Wangerooge, on the Frisian Islands out of action and free up the approaches to Bremen and Wilhelmshaven. The only Lancasters lost that day were both from 431 Squadron Royal Canadian Air Force, based at Croft. *E-for-Easy*, Mk.X KB831 and *W-for-William*, KB822, skippered respectively by Flt LT B D Emmet and Fg Off D G Baker collided; all on board both aircraft were killed.

KB839

Greenwood in Nova Scotia is the east coast base of Canada's present-day maritime patrol aircraft, Lockheed CP-140 Auroras. Since ➡

ABOVE
Operation Dodge, repatriating soldiers from Italy: Mk.I NG282 at Pomigliano, September 1945.

"BEFORE RETREATING, MYNARSKI TURNED TO THE TRAPPED GUNNER, FG OFF G P BROPHY, STOOD TO ATTENTION IN HIS BURNING CLOTHING AND SALUTED BEFORE JUMPING FROM KB726. HIS DESCENT WAS SEEN BY THE FRENCH PEOPLE WHO RECOVERED HIM, BUT MYNARSKI DIED FROM HIS INJURIES AND BURNS."

it was retired in 1965, Lancaster 10-AR KB839 has been preserved at Greenwood, as a reminder of the first Canadian post-war guardian of the seas.

Built by Victory Aircraft, KB839 was issued to 419 Squadron at Middleton St George – now Durham Tees Valley Airport – in January 1945, taking on the codes 'VR-D'. The unit disbanded in June 1945 and KB839 returned to Canada.

KB851

Lancaster X KB851 followed KB839 across the Atlantic and also served with 419 Squadron. It returned to Canada in June 1945. In the early 1950s it was uniquely converted for trials with US-built Ryan Firebee jet-powered target drones. One each was carried on specially built pylons installed underneath the outer wings. Designated Mk.10-DC, KB851 was scrapped in August 1961.

KB882

From June 1943, 428 Squadron shared Middleton St George with 419 Squadron – see KB839 and KB851. The former received Malton-built KB882 in March 1945 and it was given the codes 'NA-R'. R-for-Robert flew a dozen 'ops' with 428, its last being to Wangerooge – see KB822 – on April 25, 1945.

By June KB882 was at Yarmouth, Nova Scotia, and 428 Squadron crews readied themselves to take part in 'Tiger Force' – see HK541, earlier. No sooner had training begun for operations in the Pacific than Japan surrendered.

In the early 1950s KB882 was converted by Fairey Aviation to Mk.10-AR – arctic reconnaissance – status and it was used for test and trials work. Its last flight on July 14, 1964 saw it ferried to St Jacques at Edmundston, New Brunswick, for

display. In the summer of 2016, KB882 was taken down from its plinth while an assessment is made regarding its future.

KB889

Imperial War Museum Duxford's Lancaster X wears the codes 'NA-I' that it carried during April and June 1945 with 428 Squadron at Middleton St George, now Durham Tees Valley Airport.

Returned to Canada it was taken on charge by the Royal Canadian Air Force (RCAF) in July 1945 and by the early 1950s had been converted to Mk.10-MR maritime patrol guise.

Retired in 1965, KB889 was put on display at Niagara Falls, Ontario. Six years later it was dismantled, placed on a barge and moved across Lake Ontario to Oshawa on the northern shore with the intention of returning it to airworthiness, but this was not to be.

Warbirds of Great Britain shipped KB889 to the UK in 1984 and it was given the British civil registration G-LANC in January 1985. Acquired by the Imperial War Museum, the Mk.X arrived on a convoy of low-loader trucks at Duxford on May 15, 1986. It was restored to static display condition, unveiled as *I-for-Item* of 428 Squadron on November 1, 1994, and has been on show ever since.

KB944

The post-war Mk.10-S was the Royal Canadian Air Force's baseline bomber version of the Lancaster. The most obvious modification was the deleted dorsal turret. When the Canadian National Aeronautical Collection – today's Canada Aviation and Space Museum – at Rockcliffe, Ottawa, was selecting a Lancaster to exhibit, the Mk.10-S topped the list as it was the closest to wartime configuration.

The machine chosen was KB944, which joined the collection on May 11, 1964. Built by Victory Aircraft, KB944 arrived in the UK on March 8, 1945. It was issued to 425 Squadron at Tholthorpe in May, taking up the codes 'KW-K'. KB944 returned to Canada in June 1945. The museum also has the cockpit of Mk.10-AR KB848 for good measure.

KB976

Canadian Warplane Heritage's Mk.X 'Vera' – see FM213 – crossed the Atlantic in the summer of 2014, a feat last achieved by a Lancaster in 1975. The 1970s sortie was a one-way flight from Canada was captained by former Pathfinder Force veteran, British Caledonian pilot P A Mackenzie DSC DFC. Carrying the name *Spirit of Caledonia* and British registered as G-BCOH, Mk.10-AR KB976 had been purchased by Sir William Roberts for his expanding Strathallan Aircraft Collection in Scotland.

Malton-built, KB976 had served as 'LQ-K' with 405 Squadron Royal Canadian Air Force (RCAF) at Linton-on-Ouse during May and June 1945. *K-for-King* returned to Canada and was put into store. It was converted to Mk.10A-R configuration in 1953 and served with RCAF until it was struck off charge on May 25, 1964. Sold to the Air Museum of Calgary, Alberta, it made the last-ever RCAF Lancaster flight when it was ferried to its new home on July 4, 1964.

A plan to fly KB976 again, with the Canadian civil registration CF-TQC, in 1969 came to nothing. A year's worth of work was required to get it ready for its *second* eastwards crossing of the Atlantic on May 7, 1975. Routing via Gander, Newfoundland, and Reykjavík, Iceland, *Oscar-Hotel* arrived at Glasgow on the 20th. It touched down amid much celebration at

Strathallan on June 12; this turned out to be its last flight.

Strathallan closed its doors in September 1988, having sold G-BCOH to warbird operator and restorer Charles Church two years previously. Charles contracted British Aerospace at Woodford to restore the Lancaster to airworthiness but a hangar collapse on August 12, 1987 badly damaged the bomber and put paid to the project. Today most of the airframe is in store in Florida, as part of Kermit Weeks' Fantasy of Flight collection.

ME540

On September 4, 1949, the largest and most complex commercial aircraft ever built – anywhere (at the time) – took to the air from Filton. This was the eight-engined Brabazon, which was destined to remain a prototype; the programme was terminated in 1953. Such a huge machine, the fuselage was 177ft (53.94m), would

be vulnerable to sudden gusts, particularly in pitch. Aimed at luxury flights across the Atlantic a rough ride from a Brabazon, spilling pink gins along the way, would not have gone down well with its passengers.

Boulton Paul of Pendeford, Wolverhampton, was making a name for itself with the development of power control units (PCUs) and was engaged to come up with a gust alleviation system for the Brabazon. The solution was a long boom projecting from the nose carrying a transducer to detect gusts. An input was sent to electro-hydraulic PCUs on the ailerons which reacted automatically a quarter of a second later to damp out any disturbance.

To test this out, Boulton Paul acquired Mk.III ME540 which had been built at Yeadon – the present-day Leeds-Bradford Airport. This machine had served with 429 Squadron Royal Canadian Air Force as 'AL-P' from Leeming. The gust

alleviation device was mounted at the end of a conical boom fitted where the bomb aimer's glazing had been. Trials started in 1951 but by 1952 the Brabazon was clearly moribund and ME540 was scrapped by October of the following year.

ME559

On September 11, 1944, a force of Lancasters set off for the Soviet Union, bound for Yagodnik, near Archangel. This was Operation Paravane and, as described in Bowling 'The Beast' Over elsewhere, the target was the German battleship Tirpitz, moored in a Norwegian fjord. The units involved were 9 and 617 Squadrons and the plan was to use the Soviet base as a launch pad and return to the UK post-raid.

A number of Lancasters met with problems and had to divert or force land. One of these was Mk.I ME559 *Y-for-Yoke* flown by Sqn Ldr Drew Wyness DFC which was badly ➜

"ON SEPTEMBER 1, 1983, FRED AND HAROLD PANTON ACHIEVED A LONG-HELD AMBITION AND ACQUIRED NX611 FROM LORD LILFORD. DURING MAY 1988, IT WAS DISMANTLED AND TRUCKED TO ITS NEW HOME AT EAST KIRKBY TO BEGIN A WONDERFUL TRANSFORMATION."

damaged at Kegostrov. The bomber was abandoned and struck off charge.

Soviet ingenuity and determination would not allow ME559 to rot. The badly damaged nose section was repaired, the turret removed and parts were salvaged from other of the Paravane 'gifts'. Adorned with red stars and the tactical number 'White 01' on the fuselage, the Lancaster was used as a fast transport by the Soviet White Sea Fleet during 1945. A second Soviet Lancaster, 'White 02', has also been mooted in several sources, but nothing further is known. *Yoke* outlived

NG264

Nose-art was widespread on the Boeing B-17 Fortresses and Consolidated B-24 Liberators of the USAAF's Eighth Air Force. Adorning the forward fuselage of Bomber Command with a painting or a cartoon was far less uncommon.

Armstrong Whitworth-built Mk.I NG264 joined 150 Squadron at Hemswell in November 1944, adopting the codes 'IQ-B'. Its crew decided to paint a character from Bernard Graddon's *Just Jake* cartoon from the *Daily Mirror* on *B-for-Baker*. Captain A R P Reilly Ffoull appeared along with

(See *Five-Fifty*, page 52, for on Dodge.) One of those involved was *T-for-Tare*, Armstrong Whitworth-built Mk.I NG282 which was delivered in February 1945 from Bitteswell to 12 Squadron. By May 1947 NG282 was at 38 Maintenance Unit at Llandow awaiting the smelter.

its last RAF captain. Wyness and his crew were killed by their German captors during the raid on the Kembs Dam of October 7, 1944 – see *The Other Dams* on page 72.

ND458

Delivered to 100 Squadron in January 1944 at Grimsby – also known as Waltham – Mk.III ND458 served almost all its life with the unit. During that time, it was coded 'HW-A' and later 'HW-A²' and carried the name *Able Mabel* on the nose.

(For an explanation of 'squared' codes letters, see ED888.)

By the end of its time with 100, no fewer than 127 bomb tallies and two Swastikas denoting confirmed 'kills' by Able's gunners had been added under ND458's cockpit on the port side. All were achieved in just over 834 eventful flying hours.

This veteran was transferred to the Bomber Command Instructors School at Finningley, which moved to Scampton in January 1947. Decidedly war-weary, Able was struck off charge on August 29, 1947 at 5 Maintenance Unit, Kemble, and broken up.

one of his sayings: "We Dood It Too". (The initials 'A R P' came from Air Raid Precautions and the wardens that would enforce the blackout.) Disbanding at Hemswell in July 1945, NG264 was issued to 10 Maintenance Unit at Hullavington in May 1946 and was struck off charge on March 3, 1947.

NG282

With the end of hostilities in Europe, Bomber Command had large fleets of aircraft and vast numbers of air and ground crew with little purpose. The capacious fuselages and long range of Halifaxes and Lancasters came into their own in the repatriation of prisoners of war and combat personnel. Prisoner of war evacuations came under the banner of Operation Exodus. These mass migrations would otherwise use up capacity on ships that were needed to carry home heavy equipment, and take far longer to bring warriors home to their loved ones.

As part of Operation Dodge, a shuttle was set up in September 1945 to and from Italy. Based at Wickenby, 12 Squadron used its Lancasters to bring home 16 to 20 men at a time from Pomigliano, northeast of Naples.

NN709

Motor vehicle manufacturers had considerable experience in the setting up of vast factories and managing mass production techniques. It was obvious that such skills could revolutionise the aircraft industry – see *Building a Legend* on page 14. Austin Motors built 330 Mk.Is and Mk.VIIs from the spring of 1944 to the end of 1945.

An early delivery off the Longbridge production line was Mk.I NN709 which was issued to 622 Squadron at Mildenhall in April 1944, as 'GI-H'. After 622, NN709 joined 44 Squadron at Spilsby as *U-for-Uncle*, ending its operational service back at Mildenhall with 15 Squadron. Retired in October 1945, NN709 was processed for scrap in May 1947.

NN806

As well as evacuating prisoners of war and combat personnel – see NG282 – during April and May 1945 Lancasters of Bomber Command found a more urgent use, one that employed their bomb bays. This was Operation Manna – named after the biblical story. The people of the Netherlands were in poor state, having been subjected to

The first Mk.VII to be completed by Austin at Longbridge NX611 was kitted out to Far East standards for potential use with the planned 'Tiger Force'.

siege-like conditions by the Germans during the defence of the area in the face of the Allied onslaught across Europe. Laden with air-droppable food and medical supplies, bombers flew low over their 'targets' delivering a quick response.

Just after noon on May 8, 1945 Austin-built Mk.I NN806 of *M-for-Mike* of 576 Squadron took off from Fiskerton bound for Rotterdam, laden with supplies. Its pilot could not correct a swing that developed as it hurtled down the runway and the Lancaster, which had only been delivered to 576 on February 7, was wrecked; the crew escaped with minor injuries. At midnight, Europe was at peace and the hulk of NN806 was Bomber Command's last operational loss of the war.

NX611

The feature *Inside Job* on page 92 outlines the current status of the Lincolnshire Aviation Heritage Centre's Austin-built Mk.VII *Just Jane*. Its time as a 'gate guardian' at Scampton and at its East Kirkby home will be well known to readers.

The first Mk.VII to be completed by Austin at Longbridge NX611 was kitted out to Far East standards for potential use with the planned 'Tiger Force'. It was issued to the RAF on April 16, 1945 and spent much of its time in store.

On May 31, 1951, NX611 was taken on charge by Avro at Woodford, for maritime patrol conversion for the French Aéronavale – for more see WU-01 below.

With the serial WU-15 it was delivered to France on April 6, 1952. The last three veterans were based in the Pacific at Tontouta, New Caledonia, and in 1964 were to be replaced by Douglas C-54 Skymasters. (These were NX611, NX622 and NX665 – see page 44 for the last two.)

Newly-established British organisation, the Historic Aircraft Preservation Society (HAPS) had campaigned to take on one of these survivors and pleas were answered when WU-15 was delivered to Bankstown, New South Wales, in August 1964, ready to collect. After an epic ferry the Lancaster, then British civil registered G-ASXX, touched down at Biggin Hill on May 15, 1965. HAPS intended to operate *Double-X-ray* on the airshow circuit, but as it transpired, it was to fly only 14 times after its arrival. Its last flight was on June 26, 1970 to a hoped-for museum at Blackpool Airport. These plans came to nothing – the Lancaster plus other airframes and items were auctioned on April 29, 1972.

The bomber was acquired by Lord Lilford and it was moved to Scampton for refurbishment and display at the main entrance of the RAF base, on loan. On September 1, 1983, Fred and Harold Panton achieved a long-held ambition and acquired NX611 from Lord Lilford. During May 1988, it was dismantled and trucked to its new home at East Kirkby to begin a wonderful transformation. ➡

BELOW
Forlorn-looking Mk.VII NX664 at Wallis Island, 1984. KEC

NX622

Like NX611 on page 43, NX622 rolled off the line at Longbridge in early 1945 as a Mk.VII(FE) ready to bomb the Japanese mainland. Instead, it was ferried to 38 Maintenance Unit at Llandow and put into store. Transferred to Avro, it was prepared for use as a maritime patroller by the French Aéronavale, becoming WU-16 in June 1952.

Offered for disposal in late 1961, WU-16 was ferried from New Caledonia to Perth in Western Australia, arriving on December 1, 1962. It had been purchased by the Perth branch of the Royal Australian Air Force Association. Today, it is exhibited at Bull Creek, Perth in its own display hall, painted in the colours of 463 Squadron RAAF as 'JO-D' Digger.

NX664

Following the career of NX622 – above – Mk.VII(FE) NX664 joined the French Aéronavale, as WU-21, in August 1952. A landing accident at

Mata'utu on Wallis Island on January 21, 1963 brought the Lancaster's career to an end. Repair might have been possible, but the logistics of doing this on a remote island in French Polynesia would have been extreme and the Aéronavale had already determined to replace its veteran patrollers with nearly as ancient Douglas C-54 Skymasters.

Stripped of spares, WU-21 was left to rot, with the jungle slowly claiming it. In 1984 a mammoth recovery operation was carried out by the preservation group Ailes Anciennes and WU-21 was brought to Le Bourget, Paris, for an ambitious restoration. Work continues with the aim of displaying the Lancaster at the Musée de l'Air, which is also at Le Bourget.

NX665

As with NX664 – above – on the Austin production line at Longbridge, NX665 was also destined to serve the Aéronavale, as WU-13, and was delivered in May 1952. Along with

NX611 and NX622, it was the last of its breed in French service. On April 15, 1964 WU-13 touched down at Auckland, New Zealand, to become part of the Museum of Transport and Technology where it remains on display.

NX739

Based on Paul Brickhill's book, the film *The Dam Busters*, directed by

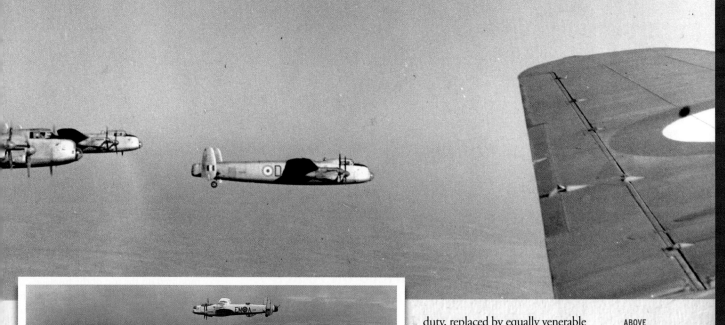

Michael Anderson and starring Richard Todd and Michael Redgrave, was released in May 1955. The bulk of the aeronautical filming was conducted at Hemswell in the summer of 1954. Four B.VIIs previously in storage at 20 Maintenance Unit (MU), Aston Down were used for the 'lead' roles. All were issued to the Hemswell Station Flight for the duration – NX673, NX679, NX782 and RT686. Filming over, they returned to storage and were sold for scrap in July 1956.

Acting as a camera-ship for *Dam Busters* was Austin-built Mk.VII NX739. Ironically, this machine had *actually* served with 617 Squadron, being taken on charge by the unit at Binbrook, Lincs, in October 1945. Its job done, NX739 was retired to 15 MU at Wroughton and sold for scrap in July 1957.

PA375

Argentina ordered 15 refurbished Mk.Is for its air force and the first of these was Chester-built PA375 which had been sent straight to storage in May 1945. With the Argentine serial B-031, Lancaster PA375 was delivered in May 1948. The whole batch had been completed by January 1949. The country was also a Lincoln customer, taking delivery of the first of 30 examples in October 1947.

PA427

As related in *Map Makers* on page 82, it fell to 683 Squadron to carry out the last operational sorties by Lancasters. The unit's PR.1s were used to patrol the Buraimi Oasis to monitor Saudi-based insurgents who were claiming the area from Oman. The Lancasters were withdrawn from this frontline duty, replaced by equally venerable Avro Ansons, in November 1953, when 683 disbanded.

While not flying in the rifle sights of Arab dissidents, 82 Squadron operated a handful of photo-survey Lancaster PR.1s based at Wyton but mostly detached in West Germany on mapping work. This was the last Lancaster squadron, if only by a matter of weeks. Working up on Canberra PR.3s from November 1953, the last sortie was carried out the following month with Chester-built PA427 credited as doing the honours. (Also serving with 82 Squadron was a certain PA474 – see below.)

PA444

Completed to Far East status, finished in the white and black 'Tiger Force' scheme, PA444 was built by Vickers-Armstrong at Hawarden in the summer of 1945. It was issued to the Central Signals Establishment (CSE) in 1946. Headquartered at Watton, CSE was involved with trials and development of ground-controlled approach procedures, radar calibration and other tasks. The large Lancaster fleet was based at Shepherds Grove in Suffolk and PA444 took on the code '4S-A'. *A-for-Alpha* was sold for scrap in December 1952.

PA474

Famed as the Lancaster operated by the Battle of Britain Memorial Flight (BBMF), Chester-built PA474's life since it returned to the air in 1967 is well known, having delighted millions of spectators. Yet it was intended to end up flightless in a museum. On September 25, 1964 PA474 was flown to Henlow

➡

ABOVE
A trio of Lancaster PR.1s of 82 Squadron over Kenya in March 1950, taken from another example. To the left is TW904 'E' and it is likely that the photo-ship or the example in the background on the left is PA474.

LEFT
A trio of 'Tiger Force' schemed Mk.I(FE)s out of Stradishall, late 1948/early 1949. In the foreground is TW900 'F-for-Fox' and unidentified 'EM-A' in the background, both of 207 Squadron. Leading is TW880 of 35 Squadron.

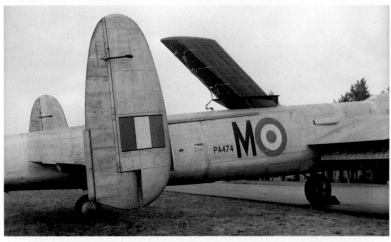

> ## "PA474 WAS ASSIGNED TO THE COLLEGE OF AERONAUTICS AT CRANFIELD ON MARCH 7, 1954. IT WAS HEAVILY MODIFIED AS A TEST-BED FOR AEROFOILS MOUNTED ON THE TOP OF THE FUSELAGE."

to join the store of exhibits for the up-and-coming RAF Museum.

With veteran Mk.I R5868 'guarding' the entrance at Scampton and earmarked for the new museum, *two* Lancasters looked like a luxury. The Station Commander at Waddington, Gp Capt Arthur 'Bootsie' Griffiths, managed to persuade the powers-that-be it would be a great idea to fly a Lancaster as a memorial. Waddington, of course, had been the venue for the Avro bomber's operational debut in March 1944. Griffiths got his way and PA474 was ferried to Waddington on August 18, 1965. After restoration it was test flown on November 7, 1967 and flown in 44 Squadron colours. It was ferried to Coltishall on November 20, 1973, and enrolled in BBMF.

But what about PA474's early days? It was built as a Far East-configured Mk.I by Vickers-Armstrong at Hawarden and issued to 38 Maintenance Unit (MU) at Llandow

on August 18, 1945 before hopping over to 32 MU at nearby St Athan in November 1946. From June to August 1947 PA474 was in the hands of Armstrong Whitworth for conversion to photo-survey status as a PR.I. In 1948 the RAF changed its designation system, jettisoning Roman numerals for Arabic ones, hence PA474 became a PR.1.

On September 23, 1948 PA474 joined Coastal Command going on charge with 82 Squadron's 'B' Flight at Benson and was given the individual code letter 'M'. In November, PA474 was one of four 82 Squadron Lancasters detached to East Africa for an extensive mapping operation. This work was completed and on February 18, 1952 PA474 returned to Benson.

Its operational life over, PA474 was allocated to Flight Refuelling at Tarrant Rushton, where it was to be prepared for a Royal Aircraft Establishment requirement. Other

than an overhaul, this task got no further as the programme was cancelled.

Instead, PA474 was assigned to the College of Aeronautics at Cranfield on March 7, 1954. It was heavily modified as a test-bed for aerofoils mounted on the top of the fuselage. Much of these trials were to investigate the Handley Page laminar flow system. The college replaced PA474 with Lincoln B.2 RF342 and the Lancaster was snapped up by the Air Historical Branch. It was taken into store at 15 Maintenance Unit at Wroughton on April 22, 1964 to await the call of the RAF Museum.

PA476

Egypt became an export customer for Lancasters in 1950, ordering nine reconditioned examples. First of these was Chester-built Mk.I PA476 which was completed at Hawarden to Far East configuration. The batch received Royal Egyptian Air Force serials 1801 to 1809.

Like many late-build Lancasters, PA476 was issued straight to storage and its first use came with 44 Squadron at Wyton, Huntingdonshire, in February 1947. The unit gave up its remaining Lancasters, becoming totally Lincoln equipped that September, and PA476 was transferred to 230 Operational Conversion Unit at Lindholme. The OCU was then the only unit training up four-engine 'heavy' bomber crews.

PB584

No.7 Squadron was based at Oakington for almost all of World War Two. In October 1940, the unit introduced Bomber Command's first 'heavy' into service – the Short Stirling. Then in the summer of 1943 the squadron began conversion to Lancasters. Mk.III PB584 joined the unit in 1944, taking up the codes 'MG-M'.

By 1945 PB584 had been retired from frontline duties and moved to Swinderby, home of 1660 Heavy Conversion Unit (HCU). As was often the case, to minimise repainting of aircraft upon change of operator,

PB584 retained its *M-for-Mike* individual code while the two-letter unit identifier became 1660's 'TV', hence it became 'TV-M'. Final service was with 1653 HCU at North Luffenham before it was issued to the bomber 'graveyard' at 45 Maintenance Unit, Kinloss and was sold for scrap in November 1947.

PD112

The Lancaster's ability to lift larger and larger weapon loads allowed Barns Wallis of Vickers to devise the 12,000lb 'Tallboy', which was followed by the scaled-up 22,000lb 'Grand Slam'. The latter was nicknamed the 'Earthquake Bomb' because it was designed to create shockwaves, on land or under water, that would topple bridges and similar structures or, as told in *Bowling 'The Beast' Over* (page 66) battleships. A direct hit was not needed, dropping the weapon close-by would produce sufficient disturbance

to bring the target down or, as was the case with the *Tirpitz*, capsize it.

The 'Grand Slam' was first dropped in anger on March 14, 1945 when the target was the Bielefeld Viaduct, east of Munster. Sqn Ldr Charles C Calder DSO DFC led 617 Squadron on the raid, piloting B.I(Special) PD112 'YZ-S', which had joined the unit at Woodhall Spa the previous month. The 'Special' denoted strengthening to the bomb bay and cut back weapon bay doors to allow carriage of the 22ft 6in (8.08m) long bomb. The 25-year-old skipper of *S-for-Sugar* was the first to unleash a Grand Slam and it impacted just 80ft from the viaduct, blowing a hole 100ft deep. By the end of the raid the middle spans of the vital rail link had fallen.

RA542

As outlined under KB822, the last Bomber Command Lancaster fatalities during World War Two took place on April 25, 1945. In the dark hours of the following morning, the final Lancaster was lost, thankfully its crew of seven sustaining only injuries. The target for Fg Off A Cox and his six comrades in Trafford

Park-built Mk.I RA542 *Z-for-Zebra* of Waddington-based 463 Squadron Royal Australian Air Force was the oil refinery at Tønsberg in Norway.

Cox and his crew were engaged by a Junkers Ju 88 night-fighter and a ferocious shoot-out followed. *Zebra* was badly damaged, but its gunners *may* have destroyed their opponent. Cox realised that he had only one option, he turned east and crossed the border into neutral Swedish airspace.

He made a successful force-landing at the Royal Swedish Air Force base at Såtenäs, north of Gothenburg. The crew's injuries were treated and all seven of them were interned. This state did not last long, 12 days later World War Two in Europe was over. The loss of RA542 represented the last of around 3,300 Lancasters that failed to return or were written off in action 1942-1945.

RE175

Coastal Command became the dominant user of the Lancaster post-war. Maritime patrol versions were the GR.III and MR.IIIs (GR.3 and MR.3 from 1948) which took over from Consolidated Liberators and soldiered on well beyond the introduction of the first Avro Shackletons in April 1951.

Wide-ranging exercises were held, mostly ➲

in co-operation with Royal Navy vessels. In mid-May 1948 Leuchars was the venue for a major Coastal Command Lancaster exercise. The resident 120 Squadron was joined by 203 and 210, both based at St Eval.

Among the Lancasters attending was Yeadon-built GR.III RE175 which was issued to 224 Squadron at St Eval in late 1946 as *P-for-Peter*. In July 1948, it transferred to 210 Squadron, also at St Eval.

Peter soldiered on until February 28, 1950 when its tailwheel collapsed at its home base. Back in the 1940s this would have been merely an inconvenience and a working party would soon have had the Lancaster

RIGHT
GR.3 RF325, the last Lancaster in RAF service, St Mawgan, October 1956.

ABOVE
GR.3 SW374 of 38 Squadron over Malta, circa 1952. Note the additional observation windows in the rear fuselage.

BELOW
Carrying an Airborne Lifeboat IIA, 120 Squadron Lancaster ASR.III at its Leuchars base, 1947.

up and running again. However, in 1950, with the retirement of the type looming and with plenty lying in store, the damage was sufficient to have RE175 declared a write off and it was promptly scrapped.

RF273

At Luqa on Malta, 38 Squadron traded in its Vickers Warwicks for lifeboat-equipped Lancaster ASR. IIIs in November 1946, adding GR.3 patrollers in 1948. In September 1953, the unit began receiving Shackleton MR.2s and the writing was on the wall for the Lancasters.

It fell to 38 Squadron to fly the last frontline maritime Lancaster sortie, GR.3 RF273 *T-for-Tango* taking the honour in February 1954. Built by Armstrong Whitworth in 1945, RF273 spent much of the late 1940s in storage and was converted from 'straight' Mk.III status to ASR.

III and then GR.III. It joined 38 at Luqa in January 1950 taking on the codes 'RL-T', which were later reduced to just the individual code as Coastal Command dropped two-letter squadron identifiers. After the wind-down of 38's Lancasters, it was ferried to the UK and sold for scrap in January 1955.

RF310

Lockheed Hudsons and Vickers

Warwicks had been adapted to carry air-droppable lifeboats for long-range air-sea rescue (ASR), from 1942 and 1943 respectively. In September 1945 ASR specialists 279 Squadron at Beccles began to receive Lancasters. These were converted by Cunliffe Owen at Eastleigh to carry that company's Airborne Lifeboat Mk.IIA and were designated ASR. IIIs. The first trials were carried out by Armstrong Whitworth-built RF310 'RL-A' in October 1945.

Although the war was over, long-range ASR over the Bay of Bengal was desirable and from December 1945 a detachment of four Lancasters, including RF310, was sent to Pegu in Burma. With 279 Squadron about to disband in Britain, the ASR.IIIs in Burma were put into the charge of 1348 Flight from February 1946.

On March 4 RF310 suffered a port engine failure on take-off from Pegu

and a series of swings developed, resulting in the undercarriage collapsing. All 11 on board got out but the pioneering Lancaster was destroyed by fire. Two months later 1348 Flight was disbanded.

RF325

Air Marshal Sir Brian Reynolds, Air Officer Commander-in-Chief of Coastal Command, presided over an emotional ceremony at St

> **"AIR MARSHAL SIR BRIAN REYNOLDS, AIR OFFICER COMMANDER-IN-CHIEF OF COASTAL COMMAND, PRESIDED OVER AN EMOTIONAL CEREMONY AT ST MAWGAN ON OCTOBER 15, 1956. ...GR.3 RF325, WAS ON HAND AND IT MADE A SPIRITED DISPLAY BEFORE HEADING OFF FOR THE SCRAP HEAP."**

Mawgan on October 15, 1956. Fifteen days previously, the last RAF unit to fly the Lancaster, 1 Maritime Reconnaissance School, better known by its original name, the School of Maritime Reconnaissance (SMR), had disbanded. Sufficient Shackletons were becoming available to take over the training of patrol crews.

The October 15 gathering was the official swan song of the Lancaster, which had first entered RAF service with 44 Squadron in December 1941. Only one of the breed, Armstrong Whitworth-built GR.3 RF325, was on hand but it made a spirited display before heading off for the scrap heap.

Formed in May 1951, the school had a complement of around 20 Lancaster GR.3s. During 1956, all were retired to 15 Maintenance Unit at Wroughton, the scene of

ABOVE
Built in late 1945 by Austin Mk.VII RT693 served with the Empire Air Navigation School as Shawbury. It was reconditioned to become the first air-sea rescue configured Lancaster for France, FCL-01, in 1954. KEC

mass Lancaster scrappings in the late 1940s. In May 1957, a total of 16 former SMR examples were struck off charge and axed, with another three, including RF325, meeting the same fate in July.

SW334

With one engine feathered, Yeadon-built GR.3 SW334 of the School of Maritime Reconnaissance was carrying out an overshoot at its St Mawgan, Cornwall, base, on May 21, 1955. It crashed on climb-out; the three crew members were injured. This is believed to have been the last Lancaster write-off in RAF service.

TW859

As related in *Map Makers*, page 82, 683 Squadron was the last RAF unit flying Lancaster in the face of possible conflict; disbanding on the last day of 1953. The unit used six Lancaster PR.1s: PA379, PA394, RA626, TW652, TW859 and TW916.

The record cards charting the life and times of RAF aircraft are a superb resource, but it needs to be remembered that the 'biographies' of its aircraft are based on *administrative* dates and not necessarily an actual physical happening. When it disbanded at Habbaniya, Iraq, the six survivors of 683's half-dozen all returned to 15 Maintenance Unit at Wroughton. Of those all but Armstrong Whitworth-built TW859, had been struck off charge as sold for scrap in November 1954. It fell to TW859, which faced the axe in February 1955, to be the final Lancaster from the last RAF frontline unit to leave the RAF's inventory.

TW910

When testing was finished on Lancaster TW910 at the Armstrong Whitworth airfield at Bitteswell, the Mk.I was delivered to 32 Maintenance Unit at St Athan, on February 2, 1946. Behind it in the almost empty assembly hall was TW911, but it did not require a ferry flight. As related in *More Than Four* on page 88, it was to be converted at Bitteswell into an engine test-bed for sister company Armstrong Siddeley.

Probably without any fanfare, TW910 became the final example to enter RAF service straight from a factory. It joined 207 Squadron, as 'EM-B', at Tuddenham in July 1946, transferring to 115 Squadron at Mildenhall in August 1949, becoming 'KO-K'. With 115 converting to Lincoln B.2s, TW910 was consigned to the scrapheap in March 1950.

VM726

Averaging 230mph (370km/h) Lancastrian C.II VM726 had clocked up 25,660 miles (41,294km) in 111 hours, 46 minutes' flying time. Captained by Sqn Ldr John Adams DFC AFC of 24 Squadron, the much-streamlined transport version of the Lancaster – see G-AGLF on page 50 – arrived back at Northolt on March 12, 1946, six days, 13 hours and 15 minutes after it had departed the base. The record-breaking out-and-back was to the Royal New Zealand Air Force base at Ohakea, near Wellington and was one of a series of 'flag waving' flights carried out by RAF Lancastrians.

While keeping an eye on the record, Adams was relaxed enough to take on board a former Australian Lancaster tail gunner at Negombo, Ceylon (now Sri Lanka) and bring him to Northolt. The veteran was hitch-hiking his way across the world for a reunion with his fiancée at Hove in Sussex!

A total of 33 Lancastrian IIs were built for long-range, high-speed communications; each capable of taking up to 13 passengers. First issued to 1359 Flight at Lyneham in early 1946, VM726 was used for VIP transport. The flight was absorbed by the specialist transport unit, 24 Squadron, at Bassingbourn in June 1946. It was struck off charge in January 1950.

WU-01

Post-war France was the largest purchaser of reconditioned Lancasters, acquiring 54 Mk.VIIs for maritime patrol, mostly from its African and Polynesian colonies. Deliveries were made between 1951 and 1954 to the French naval air arm, the Aéronavale. The last four were based in the Pacific and all survive – see NX611, NX622, NX664 and NX665.

The serials given to the maritime patrol Mk.VIIs were WU-01 to WU-54, reflecting the funding made available via the European Western Union Defence Organisation. The first of the batch, NX613, had been built at Longbridge and finished to Far East standards. It was issued to 38 Maintenance Unit (MU) at Llandow in 1945. It did not see the light of day again until June 1950 when it was issued to the Avro facility at Langar, to be readied for the Aéronavale. WU-01 was delivered in December 1951.

Not all of the Western Union 54 were 'virgins'. The last Mk.VII, WU-54, handed over in February 1954, was Austin-built NX688 and was taken on charge by the Station ➲

"On March 19, 1943 R5727 was handed over to Trans-Canada Airlines which had been tasked with establishing the Canadian Government Trans-Atlantic Service."

Flight at Wyton on July 16, 1945. The following month, carrying the codes 'GT-B' of the resident 156 Squadron, NX688 was one of a trio of Lancasters used for a tour to Brazil during June to August 1945. In September, 156 disbanded and NX688 was put into store at 22 MU at Silloth. Transferred to Avro in May 1952, it was refurbished and despatched to France.

FCL-01

As well as the Western Union Lancasters – see above – the French government acquired five Mk.VIIs for air-sea rescue work from bases in France and Algeria. All were Austin-built and from RAF stocks and refurbished by Avro in 1952 and 1953 and given the French identities FCL-01 to -05. The second machine, FCL-02, served the RAF as NX738 flying with 40 Squadron from Abu Sueir and Shallufa in Egypt as 'BL-C'.

CF-CMS

Canadian civil-registered aircraft of the period had three-letter identifiers, prefixed with the letters 'CF'. With Victory Aircraft at Malton gearing up to produce Lancaster Xs – see KB700 – former 44 Squadron Mk.I R5727 was flown across the Atlantic in August 1942 by American Clyde Pangborn to act as a pattern aircraft. Pangborn, who had come to fame as a barnstormer and long-distance

record-breaker, joined the RAF on the outbreak of war and helped to establish RAF Ferry Command.

On March 19, 1943 R5727 was handed over to Trans-Canada Airlines which had been tasked with establishing the Canadian Government Trans-Atlantic Service (CGTAS). As CF-CMS, the Lancaster was flown back to Britain on May 15 for fitment of long-range tanks, removal of turrets and installation of a streamlined nose section.

It was ferried back to Canada on July 1 routing from Prestwick, planned to be the CGTAS UK terminal, to Dorval, Montreal. The first commercial service across the Atlantic from Canada to Britain was flown by CF-CMS, with Captain R F George at the controls, on July 22. Carrying a load of mail and a couple of passengers, the Lancaster took 12 hours 26 minutes for the crossing. Taking off from Dorval on June 1, 1945 an engine fire broke out on CF-CMS and it crash-landed close by; it was wrecked but the crew survived.

CF-CMV

The success of the somewhat rudimentary Lancaster X transport CF-CMS – see above – used to start up the Trans-Canada Airlines-operated Government Trans-Atlantic Service was followed up by Victory Aircraft. A much more comprehensive

airliner adaptation was devised in 1944, designated the XPP, for Mk.X Passenger Plane. The bomb bay housed an additional fuel tank and its doors were replaced by a fairing; the rear turret was faired over and an elongated nose section acted as a compartment for mail sacks.

Headwinds often prevented direct flights in between Dorval, Montreal, and Prestwick, Scotland, but on November 5/6, 1944 CF-CMV achieved the fastest non-stop time: 10 hours 15 minutes. The XPPs plied the Atlantic route until April 1947.

Their useful life was far from over; they were snapped up by Flight Refuelling in September 1947. British registered as G-AKDO and with the call-sign *Tanker 19*, the former CF-CMV was used for air-to-air refuelling trials in May 1948, topping up British Overseas Airways Corporation Consolidated Liberator II G-AHYD. It was then transformed into a flying fuel tanker to take part in the Berlin Airlift which began in June 1948. Each XPP could carry 2,500 gallons (11,365 litres) of petrol or diesel. *Tanker 19* served throughout the operation before being retired at the company's Tarrant Rushton base and scrapped in 1951.

G-AGJI

Although Lancasters were at a premium in late 1944 Trafford Park-built Mk.I DV379 was released for trials work with the British Overseas Airways Corporation (BOAC) in November 1943, adopting the civil registration G-AGJI. It was stripped of most of its military gear, and the turrets were removed and faired over. *Jig-Item* was delivered from Woodford to Hurn on January 20, 1944 and it was used by BOAC to herald the operation of the airline-configured Lancastrians – see G-AGLF below. The first British civil-registered Lancaster was scrapped in late 1947.

G-AGLF

The Lancaster's long range and its reasonably capacious fuselage provided the basis for an interim airliner,

although its operating economics left a lot to be desired. Victory Aircraft in Canada with CF-CMS and the Lancaster XPP led the way. As well as conversions of RAF Lancasters to passenger-transport Lancastrian status, Avro also built new examples, using components and sub-assemblies from the winding down production lines.

The prototype Lancastrian was G-AGLF, which had its maiden flight at Woodford on January 17, 1945. It was issued to launch customer British Overseas Airways Corporation the following month. Lancastrians served as interim equipment for the British national airline and were withdrawn by 1950.

G-AGWH

Flying from Buenos Aries, Argentina, on the first leg of British South American Airlines flight CS59 to London on August 2, 1947, Lancastrian 3 G-AGWH *Star Dust* never arrived at its destination of Santiago, Chile. It and its 11 occupants were lost without trace, assumed to have impacted the Andes mountain range. Rumours about the nature of the flight, its passengers or its cargo, fed newspapers, magazines and books for decades.

In 1998 trekkers on the slopes of the 21,555ft (6,570m) Mount Tupungato stumbled across a Rolls-Royce Merlin engine, wreckage and tattered clothing. An expedition by the Argentine army located the entire crash site in and around a glacier. DNA testing of well-preserved remains confirmed this was the last resting place of *Star Dust*, its crew and passengers.

G-AHJW

Sir Alan Cobham's Flight Refuelling organisation began pioneering air-to-air refuelling in 1933. Post-war, the Lancaster became the ideal platform from which to continue developing the system. Chadderton-built Mk.III ED866, which entered service with 97 Squadron in April 1943, joined the trials fleet at Ford in early 1946 with the civil registration G-AHJW and the call-sign *Tanker 28*.

Flight Refuelling became a major contractor in the Berlin Airlift, which began in June 1948. On November 22 G-AHJW was routing from duty at Wunstorf in Germany for an overhaul at Tarrant Rushton, Dorset. For reasons that have never been discovered, *Tanker 28* impacted on high ground near Andover, Hampshire, killing all but one of the eight on board were killed.

G-33-2

Air-to-air refuelling has been part and parcel of military operations since the 1950s. The most versatile technique, employed the world over, is Flight Refuelling Limited's (FRL) probe and drogue system. Developed under the leadership of Sir Alan Cobham from 1933 the initial method involved grapples that captured the line from the tanker aircraft, but this was cumbersome.

The breakthrough came in the late 1940s when jets like the Gloster Meteor allowed a probe to be fitted on the nose. This could engage with a fuel line which had a 'basket' at its end that stabilised the hose and gave the receiving pilot a bigger target to aim at.

Chadderton-built Lancaster III PB372 was taken off the assembly line at Woodford and delivered to FRL at Staverton in March 1945 to become a test-bed for trials of the new system. Wearing the 'B Condition', or 'trade plate', identifier G-33-2, the Lancaster featured a foreshortened nose.

Having perfected probe and drogue, FRL decided to show just how it could transform military aviation. Pat Hornidge took Meteor III EE397 into the history books on August 7, 1949 by establishing a jet endurance record of 12 hours 3 minutes. Tom Marks piloted G-33-2 around and around the Isle of Wight, with the Meteor taking a 'drink' whenever required with ease.

I-DALR

Italian flag-carrier Alitalia purchased five Lancastrian 3s via British European Airways for use on the long-haul, multi-stage, service to Montevideo, Uruguay, which was inaugurated on June 2, 1948. First to be delivered, in August 1947, was I-DALR *Borea*, which was initially British registered as G-AHCE. Services with the Lancastrians ended in 1949. ●

FIVE-FIFTY

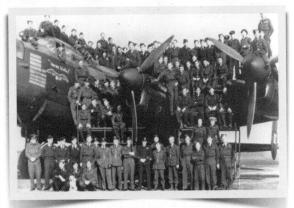

PATRICK OTTER DESCRIBES 550 SQUADRON'S TRIO OF 'CENTENARIAN' LANCASTERS AND HOW THE UNIT NEARLY HAD A QUARTET

Shortly after 20:00 hours on the night of August 26, 1944 the first of 18 Lancasters began taking off from North Killingholme, the northernmost outpost of Bomber Command in Lincolnshire. They were on their way to attack Kiel on Germany's western Baltic coast. But for a quirk of fortune that night, Killingholme's 550 Squadron might just have written itself into RAF history.

Three of the Lancasters which flew that night went on to complete 100 operations, making 'Five-Fifty' one of only three squadrons to record a 'hat-trick' of centenarians with Avro's masterpiece. That accolade would have been an unprecedented fourth but for an instrument failure on the unit's oldest aircraft.

Built by Metropolitan-Vickers at Trafford Park, Manchester in September 1942, Mk.I W5005 was part of the same batch as 460 Squadron's *George* – see the feature on page 22. It was first issued to 460 Squadron at Breighton, Yorkshire, and was still with the unit when it transferred to Binbrook in the Lincolnshire Wolds in May 1943.

After a major overhaul, W5005 was issued to 550 Squadron and took the codes 'BQ-N'. These letters had previously been worn by a Lancaster lost on the Nuremburg raid of March 1944.

WALLOWING IN THE HUMBER

Although W5005 was already a veteran, unlike some well-used Lancasters, it was not particularly popular with crews at 550. Its rate of climb could not match some of the newer aircraft, it was slow and, accordingly to some, it "wallowed around like an old cow".

For the Kiel raid *N-for-Nan*, on its 94th operation with over 600 hours on the 'clock', was allocated to the crew of F/Sgt Richard Hopman, one of five Australians in a complement that included two RAF gunners. *Nan* had struggled to the target and on the way back, as it trailed behind, it ran into a severe thunderstorm and suffered instrument damage.

Hopman later reported that rather than risk landing at North Killingholme, he elected to ditch *Nan* in the adjacent River Humber, coming down in shallow water just off Killingholme Haven, a little over a mile from the airfield. So shallow was the water that the men waded ashore and walked to a nearby gun battery from where a call was made to send transport to pick them up.

Back on the airfield Hopman and his crew were subject to much

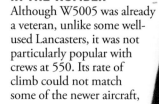

"ALTHOUGH W5005 WAS ALREADY A VETERAN, UNLIKE SOME WELL-USED LANCASTERS, IT WAS NOT PARTICULARLY POPULAR WITH CREWS AT 550. ITS RATE OF CLIMB COULD NOT MATCH SOME OF THE NEWER AIRCRAFT, IT WAS SLOW AND, ACCORDINGLY TO SOME, IT 'WALLOWED AROUND LIKE AN OLD COW'."

ribaldry for, after complaining long and hard about the state of *Nan*, an apocryphal story circulated that they had found a convenient way of getting rid of the Lancaster. It simply wasn't true but it didn't stop the jokes going around.

The Australian skipper thoroughly enjoyed all this and played up to it to such an extent that future calls to the watch tower at North Killingholme always referred to aircraft being 'upstream' or 'downstream' rather than upwind or downwind. The joke even extended to *Nan*'s replacement which wore 'SS Nan'!

VULTURE

Of the 17 Lancasters that did make it back to North Killingholme in the early hours of August 27, 1944, six would be lost on 'ops' (two of them a few days later), three would be wrecked in accidents and eight survived the war only to be scrapped, the last at Shoeburyness, Essex, in 1949.

One of those lost was a 550 centenarian, Chester-built Mk.I PA995 'BQ-V' *The Vulture Strikes!*, which was shot down on its 101st operation, to Dessau on March 7, 1945. It fell to a Junkers Ju 88 over the Harz region, four of the crew surviving.

The Vulture was the only one of 550's three 100-up Lancasters

ABOVE
F/Sgt Richard Hopman RAAF (left) and the crew of 'N-for-Nan', at North Killingholme in 1944. The others are, left to right: F/Sgt K Sharpe RAAF, navigator; F/Sgt C Stocks, bomb aimer; Sgt J Kenney, flight engineer; F/Sgt F Ferguson RAAF, wireless operator; F/Sgt Bob Sloan RAAF, mid-upper gunner, and F/Sgt R McKenzie RAAF, rear gunner.

ABOVE LEFT
'Fox' wearing daylight formation stripes on its tail. Rear gunner Sgt Frank Wright is on the left and mid-upper Sgt Leonard Wartnaby on the right.

LEFT
'Q-for-Queenie' LL837 after it ran off the perimeter track at North Killingholme early in the summer of 1944.

TOP AND ABOVE
Armstrong Whitworth-built Mk.I LL811 'Bad Penny II'.
PETE WEST

MESSAGE FROM 'THE STALKER'

Sheer joy from onlookers as 550 Squadron's 'H-for-How' drops food near Rotterdam, May 1945. COURTESY JOHN CARSON

During May 1945 'The Stalker,' 550 Squadron Lancaster 'H-for-How' took part in a low-level food drop near Rotterdam, Netherlands, as part of Operation Manna. The bomb aimer dropped a hand-written message with the 'groceries' and the crew later received a letter of thanks and this photograph from a Mr D de Krom of Puttershoek.

to be 'home grown'. It had been delivered to the squadron in May 1944 and flew operationally for the first time on a coastal battery raid on June 3/4. It led a charmed life through the summer of 1944, although PA995 did suffer some minor flak damage over Caen, and was forced to turn back with engine trouble only once.

According to Fg Off George Blackler *The Vulture* always flew "beautifully". His crew recorded 27 sorties of their tour in the aircraft, completing its 100th on the Chemnitz raid of March 5/6, 1945. Before that operation the whole of 'B' Flight was asked to assemble for a photograph with *The Vulture,* with Blackler in the cockpit. It was the following day that the Ju 88 struck.

PHANTOM

Both of 550's other centenarians had been flown by other squadrons, the best known of these being EE139 'BQ-B'. It sported dramatic nose art accompanied by the name *Phantom of the Ruhr* - see the front cover.

Delivered to 100 Squadron at Grimsby (better known simply as 'Waltham'), Lincolnshire, in May 1943 Chadderton-built Mk.III EE139 flew initially as 'HW-A' and later 'HW-R'. Its first operation was in June to Düsseldorf and it was to register a total of 32 raids before the

end of November, including five to Berlin and the attack on the research centre at Peenemünde.

It was the regular mount of W/O Ron Clark and crew, and was lucky to survive one trip to Mannheim when it was coned by the city's searchlights – a flak shell passed right through, piercing the bomb bay doors, going through the 'empty end' of the 4,000lb 'Cookie' and damaging the starboard aileron control cable.

Phantom went into a spin and fell from almost 25,000ft to 8,000ft before control was regained, only to be then attacked by a night-fighter. After evading that, the bombs were jettisoned and EE139, vibrating badly, turned for home. The crew were warned to be ready to bale out, but before the order was given flight engineer Sgt Harold 'Benny' Bennett, cut the partly severed aileron cable, and control was restored.

Back at Waltham, holes were found all over the airframe along with a 30lb incendiary bomb lodged in an engine cowling. Clark received an immediate DFC for that night's work and Bennett a DFM.

BEHAVING BADLY

Clark and his crew were not to fly the *Phantom* again for, after extensive repairs, it was one of the 'C' Flight aircraft allocated to the new 550 Squadron when it was formed at Waltham on November 25, 1943.

It is not exactly clear when it received the *Phantom* artwork but it was painted by Bennett, who had just seen the new Hollywood film *Phantom of the Opera* starring Nelson Eddy and Claude Rains at the Savoy cinema in Grimsby.

Phantom's first trip from Waltham with the new squadron was to Berlin and it was to go to the German capital another eight times. It missed the Nuremburg raid only to be damaged by a night-fighter on the night *The Vulture* made its debut. The 100th operation came in a daylight attack on Le Havre, France, in September 1944.

In November EE139 logged its 120th 'op' over Düren, west of Cologne, but its days on the front line were numbered. New flight commander Sqn Ldr Willie Caldrow

took the Lancaster to Aschaffenburg on the 21st after hearing the *Phantom* was "behaving very badly". With over 800 hours on Lancasters he felt in a position to judge how badly and, following a 6½ hour trip of "extreme discomfort", Caldrow recommended the Lancaster be taken off operational flying immediately.

The *Phantom* met the usual ignominious end, sent first to 1656 Heavy Conversion Unit (HCU) at Lindholme, Yorkshire, and later to 1660 HCU, Swinderby, Lincs. It was damaged twice and finally struck off charge in February 1946.

LUCKY 13

Credit for the longevity of the third Lancaster to top 100 operations from North Killingholme should, perhaps, be shared between the three 13 Base squadrons. Headquartered at Elsham Wolds, 13 Base – formed in December 1943 – controlled the resident units (103 and 576 Squadrons), those at Kirmington, now Humberside Airport, (153 and 166 Squadrons) and 550 at Waltham.

Another Chadderton-built Mk.III, ED905 started life with 103 Squadron at Elsham Wolds in April 1943. It arrived 24 hours after ED888

Mother of Them All which went on to record 140 operations from the airfield, before being passed on to 166 Squadron at Kirmington in September that year – see the feature *75 Lancs* on page 28.

After a major overhaul the following summer, ED905 was allocated to 550 at North Killingholme, six miles east of Kirmington. There it topped 100 operations before being retired from frontline service.

Changing identities several times, ED905 started life as 'PM-X' at Elsham with British and Belgian flags on the fuselage in recognition ➡

BELOW
'F-for-Fox' is waved away by ground crew as it prepares to take off from North Killingholme on its 100th and final operation.
AUTHOR'S COLLECTION

ABOVE
Flt Lt David Shaw in the cockpit of 'F-for-Fox' after the aircraft's 100th operation.

ABOVE RIGHT
'Phantom of the Ruhr' being bombed up with the striking nose art clearly visible, circa late August 1944.

of its first pilot, Fg Off Florent van Rolleghem. This was the work of LAC John Lamming, whose home was close to the airfield. Van Rolleghem took the Lancaster on 23 of the 26 'ops' it flew with 103 and he went on to complete two tours with the squadron, ending his flying career as a lieutenant-general in the Belgian Air Force.

Once with 166 the Lancaster became 'AS-X' and was to have an eventful life, being badly damaged by both flak and fighters during the Battle of Berlin, but each time making it back to Kirmington. During the ill-fated Mailly-le-Camp, France, raid early in May 1944, when 28 of the 42 Lancasters lost were from 1 Group, *X-for-X-ray* was attacked by a Messerschmitt Bf 110 but both gunners opened fire simultaneously and shot down the night-fighter.

CHARMED LIFE
The Mailly raid was followed by a major service at 54 Maintenance Unit at Cambridge and on its return ED905, with 36 operations to its name, was allocated to 550 Squadron where it was given the code 'BQ-F' and known simply as *F-for-Fox*. The original artwork was replaced by a crest showing a pair of fox heads, a young woman's face and a foaming pot of ale, together with the Latin motto 'Ad Extremum' (translating as 'To the Ultimate Degree') and the bomber crews' mantra 'Press On Regardless'.

Fox's charmed life continued with 550 during what was Bomber Command's busiest period of the war, the aircraft flying 62 operations between making its bow for the squadron over Gelsenkirchen on June 12/13 to November 1944. During that time Fg Off – later Flt Lt – David Shaw and his crew flew 32 sorties

"BENNETT PROVED TO BE A HARD TASK-MASTER – HE WAS DEMANDING BUT GOT THE BEST FROM THOSE UNDER HIS COMMAND BY LEADING FROM THE FRONT."

in *Fox*, on their 13th taking F/Sgt Hopman of *N-for-Nan* fame along with them for his 'second dickey' trip.

It was Shaw who piloted *Fox* on its 100th and final operation, flying with the crew of Flt Lt Joe Morris to Düsseldorf on November 2. Morris and his crew were all killed less than five weeks later in a raid on Leuna, west of Leipzig.

Once retired from 'ops', ED905 went to 1 Lancaster Finishing School at Hemswell, Lincs, briefly before going to 1656 HCU at Lindholme, Yorkshire. The following summer – August 20, 1945 – the undercarriage collapsed during a heavy landing and another 100-up Lancaster ended its days.

THREE RUNWAYS SET IN A LAKE
The squadron that all four of these veterans had in common was typical of many of those formed within Bomber Command in the last two years of the war as the assault on Germany reached its peak.

'Five-Fifty' flew just a handful of operations from Waltham before moving to North Killingholme early in January 1944 with the airfield still

far from finished. A pilot ferrying a Lancaster from Waltham recalled that, from the air, 550's new home resembled: "three runways set in a lake" and he wasn't alone in that view.

Throughout its brief life, North Killingholme was beset by problems thrust upon it by Nature – wind, rain, snow, frost and even more wind. The airfield lay just west of the Humber and close to what had been Royal Naval Air Station Killingholme in World War One. Then it was used briefly by the US Navy and the American theme was carried over to World War Two as Killingholme's nearest neighbours were the US Eighth Air Force at Goxhill – Station 345 – which was used to acclimatise a succession of American fighter groups to European conditions.

The Americans were saviours on more than one occasion, sending heavy equipment over to rescue bogged-down Lancasters. They also supplied Marston Mats, the innovative US

pierced steel planking which proved so useful in combat zones around the world.

If one word was to sum up 550 in its brief life it would be 'efficiency'. Throughout its time at North Killingholme it came top or nearly so of 1 Group's bombing tables, its rate of early returns was consistently better than most other squadrons. Its maintenance standards always came in for praise during routine visits by personnel from Group HQ at Bawtry. Even the squadron's band was judged to be the best in the Group.

Much of this was down to its first CO, Wg Cdr Jimmy Bennett, who had earned a DFC earlier in the war flying HP Hampdens in 5 Group. He was appointed to lead the squadron from a staff job at Bawtry and threw himself into the task with gusto, first at Waltham, and then at North Killingholme.

Bennett proved to be a hard task-master – he was demanding but got the best from those under his command by leading from the front. He flew whenever possible, occasionally taking new crews on their first trips.

He was determined that 550 would do its part in the bomber war, going so far as to test the all-up weight a Lancaster could take to ensure that every last ton was carried by his unit's aircraft. He said once that he knew when the limit had been reached as the wings started flexing on take-off.

Bennett was one of five men to command 550 before the squadron was disbanded in October 1945 – three of whom were lost on operations with only one surviving.

BATTLE HONOURS

The squadron's battle honours took in all the key raids of 1944-1945, Berlin, Nuremburg, D-Day, the flying-bomb campaign and the return to Germany in the autumn of 1944. Armstrong Whitworth-built Mk.I *J-for-Jig* LL811 *Bad Penny II* captained by Flt Lt Kenyon Bowen-Bravery was credited with dropping the very first bombs of the invasion of Normandy.

The squadron expanded from two to three flights, eventually with up to 30 Lancasters on strength. In November 1944 'C' Flight moved to Hemswell to re-form 150 Squadron (one of 1 Group's original units, returned from the Middle East) before building up its inventory to become a three-flight unit again.

The final operation over Germany came on April 25, 1945 when 550 provided 23 of the Lancasters which attacked Berchtesgaden – Hitler's 'Eagle's Nest' – forming part of the second wave in this symbolic rather than strategic final flurry by Bomber Command. One aircraft, *W-for-William*, suffered a technical defect but, after leaving the target area, the fault was rectified and on the way back across Bavaria it attacked the railway junction at Ruhpolding, perhaps the last bombs to fall on southern Germany in the war.

Several Operation Manna flights were made over Holland dropping supplies to Dutch civilians and later Exodus flights to Brussels to ferry home prisoners of war.

In the late summer of 1945 the squadron was involved in Operation Dodge, flying home military personnel from Italy and it was during these that it suffered its final casualties. All 26 on board Mk.I PD343 *S-for-Sugar* were lost without trace on September 29 en route to the UK; it presumably came down in the Mediterranean. A few days later a second 550 Lancaster crashed and burnt out as it was taking off from Pomigliano, near Naples, injuring three of the crew and killing two of the 20 soldiers on board.

At the end of October 1945 the squadron was disbanded on a suitably wet and windy day at North Killingholme, its crest being presented to the 1 Group AOC AVM 'Bobby' Blucke to pass on to the Air Ministry.

In the 23 months since its formation, 550 had taken part in 194 raids, flown 3,175 sorties and dropped 16,195 tons of bombs. It was one of the few units never to have been involved in minelaying, much to the relief of crews. During that time it had lost 70 Lancasters, 14 of them in crashes, with the loss of 370 aircrew.

In other words, 550 was just another Lancaster squadron. It did its job well and paid the price.

Images courtesy of the 550 Squadron Association, unless noted. The association has an impressive website – www.550squadronassociation. org.uk ●

LEFT
A 550 Squadron Lancaster bombed up at North Killingholme with a standard load of a 4,000lb 'Cookie' and incendiaries.

BELOW
Redundant Lancasters at North Killingholme in either August or September 1945.

OVER THE

A LANCASTER CALLED 'ARIES' WAS THE FIRST BRITISH AIRCRAFT TO FLY AROUND THE WORLD OF POLAR FLYING. GRAHAM PITCHFORK **DESCRIBES ITS REMARKABLE ACHIEVEMENTS**

ABOVE
'Aries' en route to Iceland.

During the first years of World War Two it soon became apparent that very few bombers were finding their targets owing to poor navigation standards, particularly at night. Also contributing to this performance were inadequate navigation aids.

To address this issue the Central Navigation School (CNS) was formed at Cranage in Cheshire in August 1942 enhance standards and train specialists and instructors. By the time CNS moved to Shawbury, Shropshire, in February 1944 bombing accuracy had improved fivefold.

The school's remit was extended to "consider navigation as a science and to carry out research into the problems of worldwide navigation". This involved a series of long-range flights, the first of which was a record-breaker, which took off from Shawbury on October 21, 1944.

The machine chosen for the

venture was a standard Lancaster I, PD328, powered by four Rolls-Royce Merlin XXIVs. It was one of a batch of 200 produced by Metropolitan-Vickers at Trafford Park in mid-1944 and had been allocated to the CNS at Shawbury on September 17, 1944.

Arriving at 38 Maintenance Unit (MU) at Llandow in Wales on September 26, PD328 was prepared for the expedition. The top turret was removed and two 400-gallon (1,818-litre) fuel tanks installed in the bomb bay. It next made a short 'hop' eastwards to 32 MU at St Athan to have the latest H2S radar fitted together with other navigation aids.

TIGER FORCE PLANS
After a series of trials PD328 arrived at Shawbury where it was given the name *Aries*, the first sign of the zodiac.

A secret document outlined the

purpose of the flight: "to visit operational and training centres in the New Zealand and Australian theatres". Five specific aims were outlined see the panel.

Undoubtedly, there was another reason for the flight. At the Quebec Conference six weeks before *Aries* took off, the possibility of sending RAF bombers to support the USAAF against Japan was raised with the Prime Minister, Winston Churchill. He was enthusiastic and soon confirmed that the RAF would provide what became known as 'Tiger Force' for the Pacific theatre once the war in Europe was over.

Although no reference was made to this in the secret document, the inclusion of investigating needs in the Pacific was not a coincidence since no other RAF forces were earmarked for operations in the area.

Some of the 'Tiger Force' reinforcements to be sent to theatre would have to fly to the Pacific via

TOP

ND LATER BECAME A PIONEER

the USA. It cannot have been a fluke that *Aries* was planned to take this likely route.

PACIFIC TRANSIT
At 10:00 hours on October 21, 1944 PD328 took off under the command of Wg Cdr D C McKinley DFC, a regular officer, a veteran of Coastal Command and one of the pioneers of the North Atlantic Ferry Service. A second pilot, three navigators, one a radar specialist, and a wireless operator made up the flight crew. Three servicing personnel and a Ministry of Aircraft Production representative were also on board.

The Lancaster headed for Prestwick, Scotland, to clear customs before leaving for Reykjavík in Iceland. The following day, the 2,300-mile (3,700km) flight to Montreal's Dorval Airport was completed.

After flying to Washington DC to brief the RAF Delegation, *Aries* set

off for a direct routing to Hamilton Field at San Francisco but was forced to divert to Omaha, Nebraska, to rectify an engine fault, which was soon made serviceable.

Surprisingly the crew had to explain the reason for their arrival to the US authorities. This resulted in a day's delay, during which clearances for the Pacific transit were obtained. Finally, at midnight on the 28th, they were able to take off on the

2,396-mile sector to Hickam Field, Honolulu, and there met with the US Commanding General.

WARM WELCOME
The flight to Auckland in New Zealand was via Samoa and was completed on the 31st. Welcoming the arrival was the Deputy Chief of the Air Staff of the Royal New Zealand Air Force (RNZAF).

After a rest during a brief

maintenance period, the crew spent the next 12 days visiting RNZAF bases.

Aries was shown off and lectures were given to squadrons and training units. McKinley and his team received a great reception, generating "exceptionally keen interest". Many local dignitaries visited the Lancaster and the crew attended civic receptions.

On November 13, 1944 PD328 was flown to Fiji, where more talks were given to the resident squadrons. Then it was on to Australia for another warm welcome.

Over the next two weeks, visits were made to both operational and training units in addition to briefings with senior Royal Australian Air Force (RAAF) and intelligence staff. The Lancaster headed for New Guinea on November 30 and then on to Darwin and Perth.

By the time *Aries* left Australia on December 11, the team had visited 24 bases in New Zealand, Australia and New Guinea.

ROUND THE WORLD

Return to the UK began with a 615-mile flight to Learmouth in Western Australia for refuelling and then a 2,680-mile non-stop stage to Ceylon arriving at first light. After just two hours on the ground, the Lancaster took off to cross the Indian Ocean heading for Masirah in the Arabian Gulf.

With just enough time to refuel and eat, the crew were airborne again bound for Cairo in Egypt, 2,352 miles away. After 90 minutes on the ground, PD328 left for Malta. As

ARIES AROUND THE WORLD FLIGHT AIMS

1 To study navigation methods and exchange information on latest developments.

2 To demonstrate items of equipment likely to be of use in the Pacific area.

3 To collect information which may assist in training crews for employment in these areas.

4 To exchange information on navigation techniques applicable to the European theatre.

5 To exchange views on navigation training generally.

well as taking on fuel, the plugs in the starboard outer engine were changed and the sand filters were removed.

The Lancaster took off at midnight to head for Northolt, Middlesex. Over France the crew received a message to divert to Lyneham in Wiltshire and on arrival were redirected to Northolt only to find the weather unsuitable for landing.

They went back to Lyneham where they were not expected and had trouble being serviced – all of this after 70 hours' continuous operation with only sufficient time on the ground to refuel and freshen up.

Eventually, McKinley was given permission to head for his base at Shawbury arriving 71½ hours after leaving Australia. This return flight was one of remarkable endurance and professionalism by the entire crew.

Some statistics illustrate the scale of the achievement. The total flying time was 202 hours covering some 36,000 nautical miles; the longest stage was 2,710 and six legs exceeded 2,200. The greatest airborne time was 15 hours, 8 minutes, on the Australia to Ceylon leg.

There were also several notable sector

achievements: UK to New Zealand in 67 hours flying time; San Francisco to Auckland in less than 60 hours elapsed; and the first Masirah to Cairo, via Aden, non-stop flight,

Australia to Britain in 71½ hours elapsed was an astounding 50 hours less than the previous official record. *Aries* had become the first British aircraft to fly around the world.

For his leadership during this unique flight, McKinley was awarded the Air Force Cross (AFC). Surprisingly, there were no awards to any other members of the crew.

POLAR EXPEDITION

A week after Aries departed on its circumnavigation, on October 28, 1944, CNS was renamed the Empire Air Navigation School (EANS). As the range and scale of operations increased during World War Two there was a growing interest in flying at high latitudes. Wg Cdr K C Maclure RCAF, a specialist navigator on the EANS staff had been studying the problems of navigation in the polar regions. He had devised the 'Greenwich Grid', a square lattice with the Greenwich meridian on a bearing

in time so a period in mid-May was chosen. There was a six-day 'window' between the 15th and 20th for the polar stages when the sun/moon fixes provided a good angle of cut needed for accurate navigation.

TRANSFORMATION

With the longest stage almost 3,900 miles, PD328 required some modifications. In April it was flown to Waddington, Lincolnshire, where the nose and tail gun turrets were replaced by smooth fairings, giving it the appearance of the Lancastrian airliner.

A Lincoln undercarriage was fitted to accommodate the increased all-up-weight. The four Merlin XXIVs were replaced with new ones. Additional fuel tanks were installed giving a full load of 4,000 gallons, increasing range to 5,000 miles.

The navigation equipment was based on the standard Lancaster

thermometer to establish the outside temperature.

Arctic survival kits, in addition to the standard gear of dinghies, parachutes and 'Mae Wests', were carried together. Specially prepared dehydrated rations were provided to sustain the crew for up to four weeks.

Aries had a crew of 11 commanded by McKinley, with Maclure the senior observer responsible for collecting data. Wg Cdr E W Anderson OBE DFC was the senior navigator. A second pilot, Sqn Ldr A J Hagger, was carried and he and McKinley interchanged positions. When not piloting, they acted as flight engineer and collected meteorological information.

Two wireless operators were carried and Wg Cdr R H Winfield DFC AFC, a medical officer and aviation medicine specialist, conducted physiological research and monitor the crew. Three servicing personnel were on board including two who had accompanied McKinley on the round-the-world flight.

80-SECOND ORBIT

Celebrations for VE Day caused some understandable disruption, and Aries was airborne from Shawbury two days later on May 10, 1945. It headed for Prestwick to refuel before setting off for Reykjavík in Iceland.

A sortie up the Greenland coast to about 75° north was made to practise navigational techniques on the 12th and to look for possible emergency landing grounds.

To take advantage of the best celestial conditions, the polar flight was planned for May 15 but unfavourable weather and high winds caused a 24-hour delay. To take off with a full fuel load, it was decided to transfer to nearby Meeks Field with its longer runway and this was done on the 15th.

After receiving a more encouraging weather report, PD328 took off at 03:00 on the 16th. ➥

LEFT
Lancaster PD382 after conversion to near Lancastrian status for the polar flight.

BELOW
Lancaster 'Aries' at Shawbury shortly before the round-the-world flight.
VIA DAVID BROUGHTON

"AUSTRALIA TO BRITAIN IN 71½ HOURS ELAPSED WAS AN ASTOUNDING 50 HOURS LESS THAN THE PREVIOUS OFFICIAL RECORD. 'ARIES' HAD BECOME THE FIRST BRITISH AIRCRAFT TO FLY AROUND THE WORLD."

of 000° from the North Geographical Pole.

In November 1944 the Air Ministry agreed to a series of Polar flights with the primary aim of studying navigation techniques under the unique conditions imposed by the high latitudes. In addition, a range of other experiments examining the behaviour of instruments particularly compasses and radar installations were to be carried out.

Other important issues for study included the collection of magnetic and meteorological data, aircraft performance and effects on aircrew efficiency.

In high latitudes astronomical navigation – getting 'fixes' from the sun and moon – was essential for establishing an aircraft's position and for heading references. The winter nights would have been ideal but preparations could not be completed

fit of H2S radar, 'Gee' and Loran. Radio altimeters were fitted, as were various types of gyro-stabilised and non-stabilised compasses for testing. Special instruments for measuring the dip as well as horizontal and vertical forces of the Earth's magnetic field were fitted together with a special

The short-lived Lincoln RE364 'Aries II'.

ABOVE
McKinley at the controls on the way to the North Pole.

BELOW
For the January 1946 Cape Town flight, PD328 was on the ground at Cairo for just 40 minutes.

Heavy middle-layer cloud was encountered and the Lancaster was still in cloud at 17,000ft where icing caused a significant decrease in speed. McKinley decided to abort the attempt and returned to Meeks Field after a nine-hour sortie.

Time was now critical, as the favourable sun/moon window would soon close. Weather forecasters suggested a more easterly route would be better, so *Aries* was airborne again two hours later. This time the cloud was less troublesome but it was not possible to take any sun or moon sights for the first four hours.

Approaching the northeast coast of Greenland at 14,000ft, the cloud began to break and the navigators obtained a series of fixes which established their position. More than 30 sun and moon observations were obtained and the final crossing of the North Pole was made down a sun position line at 02:06 hours on May 17.

The Lancaster completed an orbit of the globe in 80 seconds – by

After the success of Lancaster I PD328 the Empire Air Navigation School (EANS) at Shawbury continued long-range exploratory flights and perpetuated the name Aries for its aircraft.

Lincoln II (B.2 from 1948) RE364 was converted to near 'Lancastrian' state with a streamlined nose and tail, and was ready for service in March 1947, being named 'Aries II'. It was involved in a wide-ranging series of flights, including to the Middle East, Singapore, South Africa, Canada and New Zealand. It was destroyed by fire in a refuelling accident at Shawbury on January 26, 1948.

'Aries III' was Lincoln B.2 RE367 which joined the EANS fleet in late 1948. In July 1949 EANS was renamed the Central Navigation School. 'Aries III' was transferred to the RAF Flying College at Manby, Lincs, and served on until it was sold for scrap in January 1954. Manby continued the heritage into the jet age. In the spring of 1953 the college took on English Electric Canberra B.2 WH669 and this became 'Aries IV'. In June 1956 WH699 was replaced by PR.7 WT528 and it was named 'Aries V'.

'Aries III', Lincoln B.2 RE367 with the RAF Flying College as 'FGAW' at Manby, 1951. KEY COLLECTION

"ARCTIC SURVIVAL KITS, IN ADDITION TO THE STANDARD GEAR OF DINGHIES, PARACHUTES AND 'MAE WESTS', WERE CARRIED TOGETHER. SPECIALLY PREPARED DEHYDRATED RATIONS WERE PROVIDED TO SUSTAIN THE CREW FOR UP TO FOUR WEEKS."

that had covered 3,415 miles, PD328 made a safe touchdown. The autopilot had been unserviceable for most of the flight.

Aries was serviced over the next few days before heading west for Whitehorse in the Yukon making stops in Ottawa, Toronto and Edmonton to conduct briefings and liaison visits.

Whitehorse, which is around 6,000 miles from Britain, was Canada's most westerly airfield. Early on the morning of May 25, the Lancaster took off from its 2,000-yard (1,828m) runway with a 72,000lb (32,659kg) all-up and climbed to 14,000ft.

The route chosen took PD328 near to the Magnetic Pole and measurements on this and the previous sortie confirmed the Astronomer Royal's prediction.

Although the flight was uneventful, it proved the hopeless inaccuracy of the charts and the height data for Greenland.

On May 26 *Aries* landed at Shawbury at 12:45, after 18 hours, 30 minutes airborne. A few minutes short of 110 hours had been flown in 16 days, with three sorties in excess of 18 hours.

The expedition was a great success and was the forerunner of many others, some to the North Pole, by crews in a variety of RAF aircraft. This time, each crew member was decorated. McKinley received a Bar to his AFC and there was an AFC for Maclure and Andrews. Two of the ground crew, LACs H J B Dean and E M Wiggins received the Air Force Medal for their work on both the round-the-world and the North Pole flights. The rest were granted a King's Commendation for Valuable Service in the Air.

dipping a wing and circling the pole, the shortest possible around-the-world distance! Then it was back to Reykjavík, landing after a flight of 19 hours. *Aries* and all its equipment had worked faultlessly and all compasses behaved normally.

MAGNETIC POLE
To take advantage of the diminishing sun/moon fixing opportunities, a rapid turn-round was made, and at 04:00 on the 18th, *Aries* headed for the Magnetic Pole.

Over the Greenland ice cap, the starboard generator failed and the aircraft had to divert to Goose Bay in Labrador. With less than 36 hours of the window remaining, feverish

activity ensured PD328 was airborne again at noon on May 19.

There had been some speculation regarding the exact location of the Magnetic Pole, which the charts showed to be in the Boothia Peninsula in northern Canada. The Astronomer Royal believed it to be 200 to 300 miles further northwest.

The flight proceeded over Greenland to the Boothia Peninsula where the dip angle was found to be only 87° with the compasses still pointing northwest. *Aries* headed in that direction for a further 200 miles with the compasses becoming more erratic but fuel constraints dictated a return to Dorval, Montreal.

After an 18 hour 50 minute sortie,

OUT AND BACKS

Two weeks after returning from the North Pole expedition, the aircraft headed back to Canada on June 7, 1945. Sqn Ldr A A T Imrie DFC, RCAF and his crew flew 4,076 miles non-stop from Prestwick to Rivers, Manitoba, the home of the RCAF Central Navigation School, in 19 hours, 18 minutes.

New Year 1946 saw PD328 set off on another record-breaking flight. This time the trip involved a liaison visit to the South African Air Force (SAAF). Commanding the enterprise was Air Commodore N H D'Aeth CBE, Commandant of EANS. Captain of the aircraft was former Halton apprentice and Pathfinder leader Wg Cdr C Dunnicliffe DSO DFC. Among the crew of nine was the navigator, Captain Martin Short SAAF.

Taking off from Thorney Island, Sussex, on January 16, 1946, Aries headed for Cairo where it spent just 40 minutes on the ground for refuelling and servicing before continuing to Cape Town. After a flight of 20 hours, 37 minutes, the Lancaster landed at the Cape's Brooklyn Airport, to be met by a large crowd. This set a record for a non-stop flight from Cairo and the elapsed time of 32 hours, 21 minutes broke the existing England to Cape Town record by seven hours.

There was to be one more long-range outing for PD328. One of the recommendations resulting from the round-the-world flight was to make regular liaison visits to the RAAF and the RNZAF.

During the afternoon of August 26, 1946 Aries took off from Shawbury and headed for Blackbushe in Hampshire from where the flight to New Zealand was to commence.

D'Aeth was in command of the expedition and sharing some of the flying; the captain was Sqn Ldr J S Aldridge. A second pilot, three navigators and two wireless operators made up the rest of the crew and a servicing party of three and an Air Ministry representative were also on board.

During the planning, it had been decided to try to break the record times to Australia and New Zealand. Utilising the Lancaster's built-in long range, just three refuelling stops were scheduled using Bombay, Colombo (Ceylon) and Darwin.

The final meteorological briefing at Blackbushe on the morning of August 21 forecast heavy cumulonimbus clouds with severe icing up to 30,000ft on the intended track to the Greek island of Rhodes. It was agreed to make a diversion of 170 miles to avoid the area.

Aries took off at 12:39 and headed for Marseille, France. The aircraft was forced to climb higher than planned. When it was over the Persian Gulf it became clear that fuel consumption was much greater than expected and it was decided to land at Mauripur, Karachi.

The turn-round and refuelling were carried out in 66 minutes and then PD328 was on its way to Ceylon at 15,000ft. For the last two hours, the starboard generator failed to charge.

The night landing, refuelling and repairs at Negombo, Colombo, took 2 hours 18 minutes, after which Aries was away on the sea leg of 3,250 miles to Darwin. The accumulation of heavy cloud over Sumatra and Java made it necessary to divert from the great circle track.

Another night touchdown and turn-round at Darwin was accomplished in an hour, before Aries took off for a track of 2,873 miles at 20,000ft to the RNZAF base at Ohakea on New Zealand's North Island. It arrived 59 hours, 50 minutes after leaving England, having spent just 4 hours 28 minutes on the ground for refuelling and support.

Observers of the Royal Aero Club were present at the staging posts and three records were recognised as official by the Fédération Aéronautique Internationale: London to Karachi – 19 hours 14 minutes; London to Darwin – 45 hours 35 minutes; London to Wellington – 59 hours 50 minutes.

The crew spent the next three weeks in New Zealand and Australia attending meetings, visiting air force training establishments and giving lectures. They left Melbourne on September 24 for the return flight and arrived back at Shawbury on October 2, having covered 32,094 miles in 165 hours, 34 minutes.

Of all the Lancasters built, PD328 has a special place in the history of the type and that of the RAF. It was decided to carry on developing long-range navigation and the Aries name was perpetuated when it was given to a Lincoln in December 1946 – see the panel on page 62.

On August 11, 1948 Lancaster PD328 was struck off charge by the RAF and sold for scrap. A sad end for a remarkable aircraft. ●

"THE LANCASTER COMPLETED AN ORBIT OF THE GLOBE IN 80 SECONDS BEFORE HEADING BACK TO REYKJAVÍK, LANDING AFTER A FLIGHT OF 19 HOURS. ARIES AND ALL ITS EQUIPMENT HAD WORKED FAULTLESSLY..."

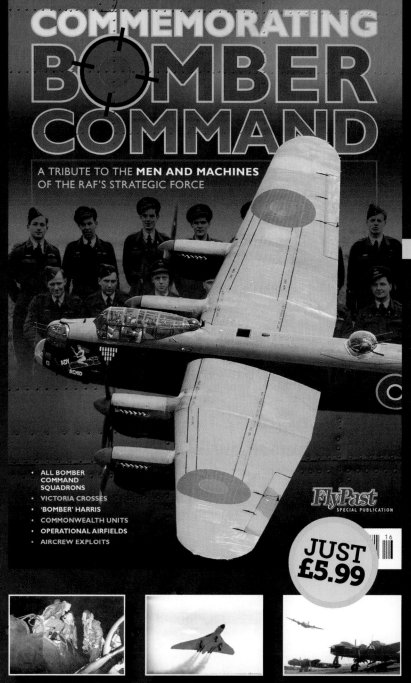

Obsessive is a word that Royal Navy high commanders would use to describe Winston Churchill's attitude to the German battleship *Tirpitz*. The great man required regular updates regarding its location and status; opportunities to neutralise what the Prime Minister referred to as 'The Beast' were never to be overlooked.

Churchill summed up the vessel's importance with typical directness in 1943: "The destruction, or even the crippling, of this ship is the greatest event at sea at the present time. No other target is comparable to it. The entire naval situation throughout the world would be altered."

The Prime Minister had good reason to respect the warship. Main armament was eight 15in (38cm) guns in four turrets. These could hurl a 1,800lb shell 22 miles (35km). There were eight 21in (53cm) torpedo tubes and sophisticated search and gun-ranging radars.

BOWLING 'THE BEAST' OVER

MASSIVE RESOURCES WERE EMPLOYED TO DESTROY THE 'TIRPITZ'. AFTER THREE RAIDS DROPPING TALLBOYS, 9 SQUADRON WAS CREDITED WITH DELIVERING THE MORTAL BLOW. ANDY THOMAS EXPLAINS

The secondary armament comprised a dozen 6in and sixteen 4in guns and, by 1944, more than 50 anti-aircraft weapons. In places the armour plate was a foot thick. Crewed by just over 2,000 men, the 42,900-ton colossus could reach a speed of 30 knots.

No wonder the *Tirpitz* dominated British naval strategy in Europe. The spectre of this giant attacking the Atlantic convoy routes meant the Home Fleet had to maintain heavy units available as a counter when they

RAF, Fleet Air Arm aircraft and Royal Navy midget submarines to destroy the battleship had managed only to immobilise it temporarily. In mid-1944 there was a weapon that could put Churchill's mind at rest and consign *Tirpitz* to history: the 12,000lb 'Tallboy' bomb designed by Barnes Wallis.

With the Allies secure on the Continent, by the late summer of 1944 Bomber Command devised a plan to strike the German

behemoth before winter closed in. This was a specialised task and two Lincolnshire-based units, 9 Squadron at Bardney under Wg Cdr Jim Bazin and 617 at Woodhall Spa under Wg Cdr Willie Tait who would take the lead in preparing for Operation Paravane.

Nestled in Kaa Fjord, a narrow, steep-sided arm of the larger Alta Fjord near Norway's North Cape, *Tirpitz* was beyond the range of a Lancaster carrying a Tallboy. There was a solution, requiring the co-operation of the Soviet Union.

RUSSIAN STOP-OVER
On the night of September 11 Tait and Bazin led a force of 38 Lancasters to the Russian airfield at Yagodnik, near Archangel. They were supported by a de Havilland Mosquito for weather recce and two Consolidated Liberator transports of 511 Squadron.

The Tallboy on Fg Off Lake's aircraft broke loose and it had to be jettisoned and the disappointed crew returned to base. Another ➔

LEFT
Lancaster I W4964 'Johnny Walker' and crew after its 100th sortie – the first 'Tirpitz' attack. Left to right: Flt Lt J D Melville skipper, Fg Off S A Morris bomb aimer, Sgt E C Selfe flight engineer, Fg Off J Moore navigator, Sgt E Stalley gunner, Sgt E Hayle gunner, Fg Off R Woolf wireless operator. 9 SQUADRON RECORDS

LEFT
Air and groundcrew give scale to a Tallboy bomb on its handling trolley. KEC

could be much better employed in the Far East.

After the loss of sister ship *Bismarck* on May 21, 1941 *Tirpitz* was moved to the security of fjord anchorages in Norway. Even while moored and being refitted, the vessel represented a latent menace. As the head of a powerful battle group, the mighty warship was an ever-present threat to the Arctic and Atlantic convoys.

From 1942 several attempts by

"...BOMBER COMMAND ORDERED A FINAL EFFORT BEFORE THE WINTER DARKNESS COMPLETELY CLOAKED 'TIRPITZ' IN ITS ARCTIC LAIR..."

Lancaster suffered an engine fire short of the Norwegian coast, but the crew extinguished the flames and gamely continued to Russia. One of the 9 Squadron aircraft was the veteran W4964 flown by Flt Lt Dougie Melrose for which the attack on *Tirpitz* would be its 100th operation see *75 Lancs* for more.

After 11 hours in the air the force arrived early on the 12th to find the destination covered in low cloud and rain with the homing beacon unavailable; only 19 Lancasters managed to get down safely at Yagodnik. Eleven more touched down at Keg Ostrov, near Archangel, but others had to use small strips or force land. Several were damaged including NF985 of 9 Squadron that Fg Off Laws managed to get into Vaskova but its port undercarriage collapsed.

All the crews had been recovered by the next day. During the first night, sleeping in rudimentary bedding, all the personnel were bitten by fleas!

FIRST STRIKE

Of the 38 Lancasters dispatched, 27 were serviceable for the raid; ten from 9 and 17 from 617. Twenty-one were to carry Tallboys and the remainder the untried 4,000lb 'Johnny Walker' self-powered roaming mine.

The attack was briefed for September 14, 1944 but was delayed because of the poor weather. On the 15th the force took off at 09:30 hours bound for Kaa Fjord, the Tallboy aircraft flying at less than 1,000ft in five waves.

All went as planned until closing on the target and climbing to bombing altitudes of between 14,000ft and 18,000ft for the final run when they found themselves off track, necessitating a major course alteration. As they approached Alta Fjord, low cloud began drifting over the waters and a smoke screen began billowing out to wreath around the ship.

In the lead aircraft Tait's bomb aimer dropped the Tallboy just before *Tirpitz* was fully covered. The sky was filled with flak bursts from both the battleship and shore batteries and the crews caught just glimpses of the vessel through the smoke and cloud.

Most of the Tallboy aircraft attacked from astern and in 9 Squadron's W4964 Melrose's bomb aimer, Fg Off Sammy Morris, spotted the stern and at 10:55 released the Tallboy from 14,900ft, noting five explosions between the ship and its protective boom.

One minute later Fg Off Tweddle's

"IN MID-1944 THERE WAS A WEAPON THAT COULD PUT CHURCHILL'S MIND AT REST AND CONSIGN 'TIRPITZ' TO HISTORY: THE 12,000lb TALLBOY BOMB DESIGNED BY BARNES WALLIS."

crew in PD377 noted a large column of brown smoke rising from the target as they released their Tallboy. Sqn Ldr Pooley's crew flying LL845 and Fg Off Taylor's in PB289 both dropped at 10:57 seeing bursts, one of which they thought might have been a hit.

Wg Cdr Bazin, captaining LM715 made two runs over *Tirpitz* and dropped, noting the smoke starting at 10:55, but could not see any hits. Frustratingly Fg Offs Dunne in LM548 and Scott in LL901 both had hang-ups.

Scott's crew attempted four runs on the target before setting course for base. Ironically, shortly before landing, the Tallboy fell through the closed bomb doors! The other two 9 Squadron aircraft dropped mines.

The aircraft of 617 Squadron also dropped before returning to Yagodnik.

The force began recovering back to Lincolnshire two days later.

BOW SHOT

Analysis of the raid confirmed one hit and three near misses. Melrose's Tallboy had hit the battleship about 50ft astern of the bow, penetrating straight through to the keel, exploding beneath allowing 1,000 tons of water to flood in.

The concussive shock from the hit and the near misses had caused severe damage to engines, machinery and systems throughout the hull. *Tirpitz* had been rendered unseaworthy and it was estimated that nine months of repair work in Germany would be needed to return it to an operational condition.

The risks of sailing slowly to Germany were deemed too great

and a conference at Kriegsmarine headquarters a week after the attack concluded: "…it was no longer possible to make *Tirpitz* ready for sea and action again". After emergency repairs, on October 15, 1944 the warship was sailed at less than 10 knots south to Tromsø to be anchored as a floating battery for the defence of northern Norway.

In London the Admiralty was unaware of the battleship's condition and so Bomber Command staff planned a further strike. Once *Tirpitz* had been located moored off Håkøya Island outside Tromsø, it was realised that it was just within range of UK-based aircraft.

SECOND STRIKE

Eighteen Lancasters each from 9 Squadron, led by Bazin and 617, under Tait, plus one from the Film Unit, flew up to Lossiemouth in northern Scotland on October 28, 1944 for Operation Obviate. Each aircraft was fitted with additional fuel tanks in the fuselage from redundant Vickers Wellingtons to give them the extra range. All were also fitted with Merlin 24s; 9's ground crews changing no fewer than 80 engines.

At 01:00 the following morning, Bazin in PD377 led 9 Squadron as the two units left Lossiemouth and flew at low level to Norway. Initially

they headed inland so the mountains would mask them from radar around Tromsø.

Nearing the target the formation climbed in clear weather. By ill luck, just as *Tirpitz* came into view there was a change of wind that blew banks of cloud in from the sea that blanketed the ship as the first Lancasters began their run ins.

Bombing 'blind', 32 Tallboys were released, but no direct hits were scored. The underwater explosion from one near miss bent the port rudder and propeller shaft, rendering further damage to the already battered warship. A 617 aircraft was hit by flak and lost an engine and force landed in northern Sweden.

Frustrated, the Lancasters began their long flight back to Scotland. One result of the attack was that a large sand bank was constructed around *Tirpitz* to prevent it capsizing. Additionally the Focke-Wulf Fw 190s of Jagdgeschwader (JG) 5 under Major Heinrich Ehrler were moved to Bardufoss, 30 miles from the anchorage to provide dedicated fighter cover.

THIRD AND FINAL

Political pressure to destroy *Tirpitz* remained and Bomber Command ordered a final effort before the winter darkness completely cloaked its Arctic

lair. Once more 9 and 617 flew to Scotland, to Kinloss and Lossiemouth, both in the grip of freezing weather.

An extremely heavy frost and lack of de-icing facilities meant that seven of 9's aircraft, including that of the CO, Bazin, could not take off so Sqn Ldr A G 'Bill' Williams led its 13 aircraft.

Thirty-two Lancasters of 9 and 617 took off at 03:00 on November 12, 1944 on Operation Catechism. They flew at low level and headed for the rendezvous point at Lake Tornea, 100 miles southeast of the target.

Two of 9's aircraft had been late taking off and did not join the attack, but the remaining 11 began climbing to bombing altitude. As the Lancasters approached the target they found the defences unprepared and *Tirpitz* lay easily visible from about 20 miles away in the clear morning sky.

Just after 09:30 they began their bombing runs under heavy fire from the ship and shore batteries. Vitally, there was no sign of the Bardufoss-based Fw 190s of JG 5 at that could have created carnage among the bombers.

Tait attacked first and over the next few minutes 28 bombs were released, achieving several direct hits. Other bombs exploded within the anti-torpedo barrier creating sub-surface cratering and had the effect of removing much of the sandbank ➔

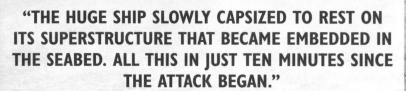

"THE HUGE SHIP SLOWLY CAPSIZED TO REST ON ITS SUPERSTRUCTURE THAT BECAME EMBEDDED IN THE SEABED. ALL THIS IN JUST TEN MINUTES SINCE THE ATTACK BEGAN."

that had been dredged to prevent a capsize.

Bombing from 16,000ft at 09:47 9 Squadron's Flt Lt Lake in PB696 saw five bombs fall with one exploding 50 yards off the bow, another slightly undershot the centre of the ship, a third 30 yards off the stern and two more overshoot by about 150 yards. His rear gunner, F/Sgt Parkes: "considers own bomb hit the ship as a big explosion and fire followed immediately".

Flying PD368, Sqn Ldr Williams saw: "Very near miss on starboard side aft seen just before bombing and about three other bombs seen to burst close to the ship. One hit as a column of smoke enveloped the ship and its guns stopped firing."

The first bomb had hit between the forward 'Anton' and 'Bruno' 15in gun turrets and penetrated the armoured deck, but failed to explode. A second entered just aft of the funnel, blowing out a large hole. With this, *Tirpitz* took on a significant list.

A third impacted on the side of the aft 'Caesar' 15in turret causing further flooding and increased the list. Seconds later a violent explosion blew out the turret, probably as the magazine ignited.

The huge ship slowly capsized to rest on its superstructure that became wedged in the seabed. All this in just ten minutes since the attack began.

TOPPLED BY 9

The Lancasters headed home, although LM448 flown by Fg Off Coster had been hit by flak and force landed at Överkalix in northern Sweden.

Both squadrons claimed hits but subsequently it was ascertained that it was the Tallboy dropped by the 9 Squadron Lancaster flown by Tweddle's crew, LM220 that struck

the mortal blow. Douglas Tweddle, who was awarded the DFC for his part, said afterwards: "We flew north at only 1,000ft to get to the Norwegian coast below radar. Then we went into a climb over the coast to a rendezvous about 80 miles from our target.

"My aircraft was one of the last over the battleship and we were still over the area when we saw *Tirpitz* start to roll over. I knew before we got back to Lossiemouth when we were shown pictures taken later by a Spitfire that the *Tirpitz* had been sunk."

There was great relief that the brooding threat from the 'The Beast' had finally been eradicated after more than two years of sustained effort. ●

ABOVE
Lancasters of 9 and 617 Squadrons including LM715 on the left that was flown by the CO Wg Cdr Bazin sitting at Yagodnik on September 11, 1944 awaiting the weather to clear for the first effort on 'Tirpitz'.
M HAMILTON

RIGHT
Bombing plot from Sqn Ldr Williams's aircraft, November 12, 1944.
VIA AUTHOR

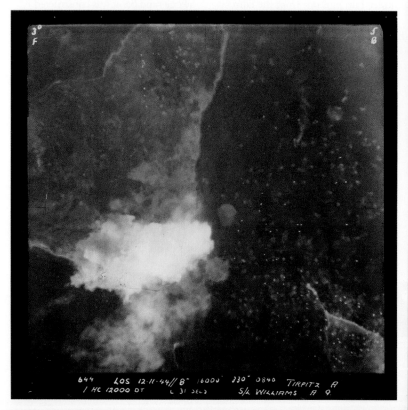

AVIATION SPECIALS

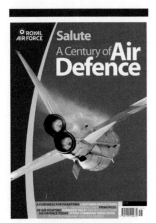

RAF SALUTE
A CENTURY OF AIR DEFENCE
Marks the 80th anniversary of the formation of RAF Fighter Command

£5.99 inc **FREE** P&P*

KOREAN WAR
The story of North Korea's invasion of South Korea through interviews and historical analysis.

£6.99 inc **FREE** P&P*

SPITFIRE 80
Tribute to Britain's greatest fighter and possibly the best known combat aircraft in the world.

£3.99 inc **FREE** P&P*

VULCAN
A tribute to the most challenging and complex return-to-flight project ever.

£3.99 inc **FREE** P&P*

BATTLE OF BRITAIN SALUTE
Commemorating the RAF's role in one of history's greatest air battles.

£5.99 inc **FREE** P&P*

BOMBER COMMAND
An incredible salute to the men, machines and exploits of Bomber Command.

£5.99 inc **FREE** P&P*

GULF WAR
A must-have for those seeking to understand the conflict that changed the shape of warfare.

£3.99 inc **FREE** P&P*

RAF OFFICIAL ANNUAL REVIEW 2017
Behind the scenes insight into the aircraft, equipment and people of one of the world's premier air forces.

£5.99 inc **FREE** P&P*

AVIATION SPECIALS

ESSENTIAL reading from the teams behind your **FAVOURITE** magazines

HOW TO ORDER

 **OR**

PHONE
UK: 01780 480404
ROW: (+44)1780 480404

FREE Aviation Specials App

Simply download to purchase digital versions of your favourite aviation specials in one handy place! Once you have the app, you will be able to download new, out of print or archive specials for less than the cover price!

IN APP ISSUES **£3.99**

THE OTHER DAMS

ANDY THOMAS DEMONSTRATES THAT AS WELL AS THE FAMOUS 617 SQUADRON RAID, OTHER GERMAN DAMS WERE IN BOMBER COMMAND'S SIGHTS

Of all its Battle Honours, possibly the most revered by the Royal Air Force are those of 'Battle of Britain 1940' and 'The Dams'. To most, the latter refers to the stunning raid in May 16/17, 1943 by the Lancasters of 617 Squadron that breached the Möhne and Eder Dams and damaged the Sorpe.

But 617 does not have exclusivity on this honour, 9 Squadron also has claim to it. After the war the criteria for the award of 'The Dams' Battle Honours was defined as: 'For squadrons participating in the operations for breaching the Möhne, Eder, Sorpe and Kembs Dams, May 1943 to October 1944.' But there were other attacks on great German dams after these dates.

As is well known, although initially formed specifically for the Dams Raid, it was afterwards decided to retain 617 Squadron for operations requiring particular precision and a high degree of

ABOVE
Flt Lt Kit Howard, aged 22, and his crew died on the Kembs attack. VIA M POSTLETHWAITE

skill. Beyond May 1943 the unit replaced its losses and retrained before returning to operations.

Its role changed significantly to that of high-level precision bombing using the Stabilised Automatic Bomb Sight (SABS) that paved the way for the 12,000lb 'Tallboy' earthquake bomb. This was another invention of Dr Barnes Wallis and became operational with 617 in mid-1944 just after the invasion of France. During July 1944 Wg Cdr J B 'Willie' Tait assumed command of 617 and continued its specialised tasks.

LETHAL TORRENT
By early October the Wehrmacht had retreated into Germany. The Americans had halted on the River Rhine near Belfort to regroup before crossing this last great natural barrier.

At Supreme Allied Headquarters there was real concern that the flood control gates on the Kembs Barrage, just north of Basle, might be blown by the Germans just as US troops began to cross the Rhine. This would turn the mighty river into a torrent that could at best delay the Allied advance,

at worse cause an untold number of casualties.

It was deemed essential that the gates be destroyed before the assault, which could then begin after the surge had passed. While it was thought that the 'Upkeep' bouncing bomb was the most suitable weapon, there was insufficient time to train the new crews in its delivery.

The attack on the Kembs Barrage was to be conducted in daylight from low level using the Tallboys. During planning it became evident that this was a difficult and dangerous task as the barrage was heavily defended. A concurrent high-level attack was also planned to try to split the defences.

OPENING THE GATES
Thirteen aircraft were allocated for the raid. The first wave of seven Lancasters was to conduct the high-level attack and began taking off from Woodhall Spa, Lincolnshire, shortly after 13:00 hours on October 7, 1944. The low-level element, led by Tait at the controls of EE146, departed shortly afterwards.

Under heavy escort the 13 Lancasters began their approach to the target soon after 16:30. The high-

level section began bombing at 16:44 when Fg Off Watts' crew released the Tallboy from LM485. Four more bombs quickly followed as the six low-level aircraft led by Tait ran in at 600ft (182m) in marginal weather and into intense ground fire.

Tait's Tallboy was dropped at 16:51 just ten yards (9m) short of the target sluice gate. When the delay fusing activated, it exploded, breaching the barrage.

Sqn Ldr Drew Wyness in NG180 followed, but his Lancaster was badly hit though he continued and released the weapon. His aircraft staggered away and Wyness managed to ditch it in the Rhine a little way downstream. The crew survived the ditching, were captured and shot out of hand by German troops.

Within four minutes the other four crews had successfully bombed, but three of these aircraft also suffered flak damage. In LM482 Flt Lt Kit Howard, having braved the hail of fire, decided that he was not properly lined up, so gallantly flew round for a second attempt.

The aircraft was hit in the starboard wing, which started an uncontrollable fire that quickly spread. Lancaster ➔

BELOW AND BOTTOM LEFT
The Kembs Barrage before and after the raid of October 1944.
BOTH RAF SCAMPTON

"617 SQUADRON'S ROLE CHANGED SIGNIFICANTLY TO THAT OF HIGH-LEVEL PRECISION BOMBING USING THE STABILISED AUTOMATIC BOMB SIGHT THAT PAVED THE WAY FOR THE 12,000lb TALLBOY EARTHQUAKE BOMB."

ABOVE
The Standard of 9 Squadron showing the Battle Honour for 'The Dams'.
RAF LOSSIEMOUTH

ABOVE RIGHT
Craters on the Sorpe Dam showing the accuracy of the 9 Squadron attack. AHB

BELOW
Wg Cdr Willie Tait and his crew in front of Lancaster I EE146, November 11, 1944.
617 SQN RECORDS

LM482 dived into the ground and exploded, killing all the crew.

Despite the losses, the attack had been successful and a major obstacle to Allied plans for the advance into Germany had been removed. This, like subsequent attacks on water infrastructure, was in support of the land offensive rather than to damage enemy industrial output.

SORPE REVISITED

Shortly after the successful Kembs raid a request to attack the Sorpe Dam, which 617 had attacked and damaged the previous year, was made. The dam was constructed of a concrete core flanked on both sides by massive earth banking and was deemed suitable to attack with Tallboys.

Based at Bardney, Lincolnshire, 9 Squadron under Wg Cdr Jim Bazin was also armed with the Tallboy, although it did not have the SABS capability. This unit was tasked with

"...THE FIRST OF 16 TALLBOY BOMBS FELL OVER THE NEXT FOUR MINUTES. SEVERAL OF THEM STRUCK THE MASSIVE STRUCTURE LEAVING CRATERS UP TO 50ft DEEP AND NEARLY 100ft ACROSS."

striking at the Sorpe.

Early on October 15, 1944 Bazin in LM715 led 18 Lancasters. One of these was flown by Fg Off Edward Bates, who was celebrating his 31st birthday!

Under heavy fighter escort from seven squadrons of North American Mustangs, the squadron approached the target shortly after 09:00 at 14,000ft and at 09:25 the first of 16

Tallboy bombs fell over the next four minutes. Several of them struck the massive structure leaving craters up to 50ft deep and nearly 100ft across.

Many ring-shaped cracks appeared in the dam. On the crest the concrete was smashed open with two large craters, another pushing the wall aside. Despite the accuracy of 9's bombing, this

second attack was also unsuccessful, although the water level in the Sorpe reservoir had to be lowered to ease the pressure on the structure.

REDUCING THE PRESSURE

The potential for a devastating flood against advancing troops returned as the US 1st Army advanced into the Eifel mountains to the southeast of Aachen. It was feared that that the Urft and the Schwammenauel Dams on the River Roer might be used to halt their advance across the river near Jülich. Again, a pre-emptive breaching was requested.

Bomber Command mounted several conventional bombing attacks against the dams but without success. This was hardly surprising as the Urft, southwest of Cologne was a massive 160ft-high masonry structure.

The first attack on December 4, 1944 was flown by 27 Pathfinder Lancasters from 8 Group and did destroy the top of the dam, but failed to breach it. The following day 56 Lancasters from 3 Group struck at the Schwammenauel, but thick cloud meant that just two aircraft bombed.

The Urft was targeted again on the 8th by 205 Lancasters from 5 Group. This time, 9 and 617 Squadrons participated with Tallboys.

The five aircraft from 9 were led by Flt Lt Watkins in PB368 while Tait, flying EE146, headed 19 Lancasters of 617. On arriving in the target area at 09:00 they found complete cloud cover and, after orbiting for some time, there were insufficient breaks so Tait aborted the operation.

In the crowded sky over the target Mk.III LM637 of 630 Squadron, skippered by Flt Lt R F Lewis, collided with another Lancaster and crashed. The other aircraft involved managed to return to base. There was just one survivor from the Lewis crew.

Three days later 5 Group sent 233 Lancasters to have another attempt at the Urft and, once more, Tallboy aircraft from both 9 and 617 were included. Tait again led 617, taking off from Woodhall Spa soon after midday.

From ED763 Flt Lt Oram dropped the first Tallboy at 15:19 and others were soon bursting around the dam. Flt Lt Goodman's rear gunner saw their bomb dropped from NF992 and burst near the centre of the spillway. Ten minutes later Tait's bomb aimer released their weapon and it hit the middle of the structure. There was little flak and all of 617's aircraft returned safely.

Although the dam was not breached, it was so damaged that the Germans were forced to lower the water level, so reducing the pressure. The threat of a potential flood was removed. The next day the Supreme Headquarters Allied Expeditionary Force halted such tactical operations by heavy bombers as they were diverting effort from strategic targets. The era of attacking the great dams of Germany had ended. ●

TOP
A 9 Squadron Lancaster running in over a target, 1944.
AUTHOR'S COLLECTION

ABOVE LEFT
Fg Off Carr with bomb aimers F/Sgts Fisher and Flynn of 9 Squadron with Tallboys.
9 SQUADRON RECORDS

ABOVE
The Urft Dam showing damage after the attacks on December 4, 1944.
617 SQUADRON RECORDS

HALIFAX VERSUS

LANCASTER

FLIGHT ENGINEER HUMPHREY PHILLIPS RECALLS HIS EXPERIENCES WITH BOTH THE AVRO AND HANDLEY PAGE HEAVIES TO SEAN FEAST

ABOVE
The Lancaster's bomb bay offered an incredible variety of munitions. As well as a smaller bomb bay, the Halifax had weapon cells in the centre section. These severely hampered weapon size and permutations.
KEY COLLECTION

While Bomber Command was thankful for the introduction of the four-engined 'heavies' into its armoury, these mammoths presented a number of challenges for the men at the Air Ministry and the operational squadrons. The Short Stirling had its service debut with 7 Squadron at Leeming, Yorkshire, in August 1940. Leeming was also the venue for the first Handley Page Halifax, joining 35 Squadron in November 1940. It was another 11 months before 44 Squadron was able to inaugurate the Lancaster, at Waddington, Lincolnshire.

One problem was how to convert both experienced and novice pilots from two engines to four, without taking them away from frontline duties for longer than was necessary and with only a limited number of new aircraft at their disposal. A second was how to monitor and manage

the additional engines and complex systems that were now clearly beyond the scope of the man responsible for flying the aircraft.

Initially, conversion training was achieved through the creation of dedicated Conversion Flights within each squadron. These were designated accordingly, for example 44 Conversion Flight was a part of 44 Squadron, 103 Conversion Flight was based at Elsham Wolds, Lincolnshire, working up on Halifaxes for 103 Squadron.

Instructors who had already trained on the type were allocated to converting their colleagues, each individual pilot having to wait patiently for his turn. As more aircraft became available, the Conversion Flights were merged into homogenous Conversion Units (and later designated Heavy Conversion Units HCUs) to which pilots and crews were sent immediately after Operational

Training Unit and before posting to a squadron.

Solving the increased complexity of the heavies was more convoluted in its gestation and confused in its birth, but ultimately led to the creation of a new aircrew category: the flight engineer. Initially, flight engineers were taken from the ranks of existing airmen considered to have the necessary skills.

A NEW BREED

Volunteers from among a pool of highly skilled flight mechanics were recruited, supplementing their talents with a six-week gunnery course at which point they were considered 'qualified'. While the training evolved considerably throughout World War Two, in the beginning it was at best ad hoc, with not a little invention along the way.

Humphrey Phillips was one of this new 'breed' of aircrew who had been an apprentice motor mechanic before the war. Not surprisingly, he volunteered first for training as a flight mechanic, and upon qualifying near the top of his course, was given further training to become a more exalted Fitter II E the 'E' standing for 'engines'.

Humphrey was retained as an instructor at St Athan, Wales, before seeing the Air Ministry Order calling for further volunteers to become flight engineer aircrew. After some additional gunnery training, Humphrey was posted to 102 Squadron, and immediately attached to the unit's 102 Conversion Flight, commanded by Sqn Ldr Peter Robinson DFC.

Thus began a period of almost two years for Humphrey as an instructor. He rose from the rank of corporal (this was before the days that all aircrew held the minimum rank of sergeant) in charge of flight engineers

before being commissioned and appointed flight engineer leader.

His early career reflects the transitional period for training at that time. It comprised a series of short attachments, often less than a fortnight, to the Conversion Flights of 102, 103, and 460 (RAAF) Squadrons.

Humphrey's instruction included a brief attachment to 1652 CU at Marston Moor, Yorkshire, to take part in the 'Thousand Bomber' raids on Cologne (May 30/31, 1942) and Essen (June 1/2). He had a ten-day spell at Avro, Woodford, to train specifically on the Lancaster and complement his existing knowledge on the Halifax acquired during a brief spell at English Electric at Samlesbury, near Preston.

Humphrey then became a founding member of 1656 Conversion Unit (CU), headquartered at Lindholme, Yorkshire. The unit was formed in

October 1942 by amalgamating 103 and 460 Conversion Flights under the command of Wg Cdr Arthur Hubbard DFC.

SCROUNGE AND ADAPT

As such, Humphrey has something of a privileged view of the four-engined heavies of that time, and particularly the Halifax and the Lancaster. He also has first-hand knowledge of the dangers of converting, not only for the novice crews, but also the experienced instructors (pilots and flight engineers)

obliged to go along for the ride!

His logbook is populated by such names as 'Harry' Drummond, 'Daddy' Lashbrook, 'Shorty' Fahey, 'Willie' Caldow, 'Bluey' Graham and other such notable pilots of their time whose contribution in transitioning new crews has perhaps not yet been fully recognised.

Humphrey recalled: "The task of training at HCU was divided into ground instruction and instruction in the air. Ground instruction was primarily lectures for all the crew, sometimes together, and sometimes split into their individual specialisms, on such things as day and night landings, three-engined flying procedures, and emergency drill. As well as the lecture halls, we had rooms equipped with different parts of the aircraft so we could better illustrate how systems worked."

Section leaders were left to their own devices in respect of training

aids: "We would scrounge parts from crashed aircraft before the official 'salvage' teams moved in. This enabled me, with the help of our chief ground instructor, to commission the construction of a working, diagrammatical fuel system and a fully working undercarriage mechanism so that I could demonstrate the functions of the locking mechanism."

CIRCUITS AND BUMPS

It was in the air, however, that the fun really began.

Humphrey continued: After a familiarisation flight, the pilots were trained in take-offs and landings referred to as 'circuits and bumps' two at a time, until both pilots were safe to perform solo. Their dual training also included learning how to handle the aircraft with three engines.

"When it came to the solo, the flying instructor retired to the control tower but the staff engineer which could be me remained with the aircraft. It was during some of these solos that I had my hairiest moments.

"One night I was with two trainee pilots practising circuits and bumps and after the first circuit we landed and taxied to the end of the runway for a second take-off. The pilot began running up ➲

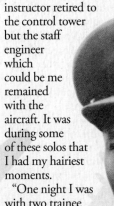

some 'gremlin' in the ailerons and that made us understandably cautious. It was, therefore, in a thoughtful mood that we made our way out to dispersal via the flight office, where Willie signed the Form 700 [servicing record].

"We did our external checks and clambered aboard, wondering what we might find. All seemed to be in order and we began our starting, run-up and cockpit drill, blissfully ignorant of the danger at hand."

Everything seemed normal as they

ABOVE RIGHT
Halifaxes coming off the assembly line at English Electric, Samlesbury. Humphrey Phillips visited this and the Avro factory at Woodford. KEC

RIGHT
Lancaster fuel system teaching aid devised and used by Humphrey Phillips at 1656 CU.

the engines against the brakes while I kept an eye on the instrument panel.

"To my horror I could see that there was no oil pressure on the starboard inner engine. Neither pilot had noticed that the engine had, in fact, stalled the pilot is supposed to check these instruments as he opens the throttles and they were about to try to take off on three engines.

"On another occasion on another solo, as the second pilot responded to the instruction 'undercarriage down', we had a red light to show that the starboard wheel was not down and locked.

"We thus went through the various emergency routines, but the wheel remained obstinately stuck. As we circled at a thousand feet, the pilot called the control tower and the instructor 'Daddy' Lashbrook asked whether we had checked the up-locks. Making my way aft I was rather surprised to find one of our staff wireless 'ops' on the rest bed, making up his monthly hours.

"The up-lock control emerges from the fuselage side at the foot of the bed, and on this particular aircraft it had been fitted with an extension bar to make it accessible if overload fuel tanks were fitted. Our 'intruder' had pulled the bar out on which to rest his feet! No sooner had he taken his feet away then I was able to push the bar to the 'unlocked' position and the green light blinked to tell as the undercarriage was down."

TIRED OLD CRATES
While both of these incidents were experienced flying a Halifax, it was during a routine air test in a Lancaster that Humphrey was the closest to coming to grief.

"A well-known danger among trainee

"SELDOM DID WE GET OUR HANDS ON ANYTHING 'NEW'; MORE USUALLY THEY WERE SECOND-HAND, TIRED OLD CRATES WHOSE AIRFRAMES AND ENGINES HAD BEEN FLOGGED BEYOND ENDURANCE."

pilots and instructors throughout the war was the quality and reliability of aircraft in which we flew. Seldom did we get our hands on anything 'new'; more usually they were second-hand, tired old crates whose airframes and engines had been flogged beyond endurance. Serviceability was an issue, despite the heroic efforts of the groundcrews who, it seemed, were fighting a daily battle they could rarely win.

"*A-for-Apple* was a 'rogue' Lancaster that had all the hallmarks of being a squadron cast-off. My pilot, 'Willie' Caldow, and I received instruction to fly the initial air test prior to putting the aircraft into service.

"We had been told that she had

taxied out and started the take-off run. The Lancaster steadily picked up speed along the runway until they had about 125mph (201km/h) indicated airspeed and the tail came up.

"Willie appeared to be lugging on the control column with unusual vigour as he wound back furiously on the elevator trim. He had a somewhat puzzled look on his face as he panted out: 'It doesn't want to come unstuck'.

"At last, long past the point of no return, the aircraft reluctantly left the runway and we were finally airborne and in a shallow climb. Quickly this changed to quite a steep climb with Willie now pushing hard on the control column to keep the nose down to build our airspeed and prevent us from stalling. He was furiously winding the trimmer forward again with his right hand to take off all of the trim he had used to get us in the air."

The pilot remained concerned, though he had now gained sufficient control to produce a normal rate of climb.

"It was clearly taking it out of him physically as he instructed me to pull both the wheels and the flaps up to reduce drag and cause a nose-down change of trim. Having complied, he told me that the elevators felt locked and that he had only managed to gain control by an excessive use of the elevator trim control, which I had seen."

DOWN TO EARTH

"It was as we reached a thousand feet that the fun started. Endeavouring to make the first turn to port, on to our left-hand circuit of the station, Willie was again having to use considerable physical force to get the aircraft to do anything.

"He managed to gasp out a somewhat cryptic message that he felt that the ailerons were now locking, and began frantically winding the aileron trimmer to compensate. It was getting desperate now: He shouted: 'Think! What the hell can it be?'

"I tried to force my mind to work logically and systematically through the possibilities affecting both elevators and ailerons being overridden by the trim tabs. I could think of

nothing, but my thoughts were interrupted by Willie's shout that we were not going to make it back to the runway. We needed to find a place to put down, and quickly."

At this point the aircraft had achieved a semblance of stable flight. They were able to maintain altitude and speed, and were flying parallel with the runway on the down-wind of the circuit with good visibility. Humphrey was therefore able to see the ground ahead and to starboard quite clearly, but alas neither of them could see anything remotely like an adequate piece of flat land on which to make an emergency landing.

"A minute or two passed and we were nearing the next turn to port for the crosswind short leg. Somewhat more composed, Willie quickly briefed me on assisting him on the approach and landing. Between us we somehow managed to bring the mighty beast back down to earth and even pulled off a creditable landing, all things considered.

"Willie was exhausted. We taxied the Lancaster back to dispersal without uttering a word."

IMPOSSIBLE

"We spoke briefly about the symptoms and possible causes, and agreed that the problem was a complete locking of the aileron controls. The other flying controls, and especially the elevators, had also felt odd.

"In the sergeants' mess I joined the only table that was still occupied. A gaggle of my fellow engineers were

chatting to a stranger. He was not, as it happens, just 'another engineer', but rather an operational 'type' from a neighbouring squadron.

"One of my friends commented on my somewhat harassed demeanour, and I was encouraged to give an account of what had happened. Naturally I expected some sympathy, but instead my story was greeted with looks and expressions of disbelief from all except the stranger.

"With a cynical and rather patronising tone he said: 'It's obvious old chap. You two clots had 'George' in.' His statement was followed by a moment or two of ominous silence, during which time my mind raced over the relevant facts and I had a strange feeling in the pit of my stomach.

"With something of a cold sweat I spluttered: 'Impossible. Firstly, all of our George controls are wired 'out'; and secondly, it would have been impossible to fly the kite manually with George engaged. We would not be here to tell the tale.'

"My statement provoked quite a heated discussion, lasting some minutes. I allowed the others to talk over themselves but made no further contribution to the debate.

"Instead, I proceeded to bolt my lunch and beat a hasty exit. Grabbing my bike from outside of the mess, I pedalled furiously back to dispersal.

"Climbing hurriedly into the aircraft and making my way forwards, one glance in the cockpit revealed the awful truth: both of George's ➡️

"...IT GAVE YOU GREATER CONFIDENCE WHEN YOU WERE IN THE AIR. YOU NEVER HEARD OF A LANCASTER FALLING OUT OF THE SKY FOR NO KNOWN REASON, BUT THE SAME COULD NOT ALWAYS BE SAID OF THE HALIFAX."

clutches were 'in'; the automatic pilot was fully engaged!"

Willie and Humphrey had just achieved what everyone had previously believed impossible. Humphrey later phoned Willie and thanked him for saving his life.

TOO FUSSY

Given Humphrey's experience on both types, how did the Halifax and the Lancaster compare?

"The Halifax was a fairly crude aircraft, whereas the Lancaster was more refined in every sense. The Halifax had comparatively poor aerodynamics and certainly didn't fly as well on three engines. The problems with its tail assembly were well documented at the time – and since – and they were constantly modifying the fins to find the answer.

"She could flip into a rudder stall far too easily and often, catching out all but the most experienced pilots and even some of those lost their lives. There were more technical faults with a Halifax as well as specific 'quirks', such as the problems we had with the tailwheel; it was even possible for a Halifax to take off and leave its tail

wheel on the runway.

"When we first started flying the Halifax, engineers were instructed to open the cross-feed cock for the fuel on take-off, and close it immediately afterwards. The idea was that this would ensure that the flow of fuel was constant to all engines during one of the most critical phases of flight.

"Unfortunately, the opposite was the case, and leaving the cross-feed cock open actually starved two of the engines of fuel causing the aircraft to crash. I remember clearly the urgent instruction we received to halt this practice with immediate effect.

"But that was part of the problem with the Halifax: it was too fussy; too unnecessarily complicated. There were too many fuel tanks, the Halifaxes we flew had six fuel tanks in each wing. The hydraulics had too many remedies, and too many things

hydraulic system was easier and the undercarriage less complicated.

"There was far less to go wrong and therefore it gave you greater confidence when you were in the air. You never heard of a Lancaster falling out of the sky for no known reason, but the same could not always be said of the Halifax."

Of course, Humphrey says, that's not to say that the Lancaster was perfect. It was not.

"The flight engineer's position in a Lancaster was as uncomfortable as it was in the Halifax, and ergonomics had not been uppermost in the designer's mind. The flight engineer panel in a Halifax was actually rather well laid out, with the fuel tank gauges, oil temperature gauges, engine temperature gauges etc all logically displayed.

"The Lancaster flight engineer's position was rather more 'Heath Robinson', behind and to the starboard of where you stood or sat if you were lucky and so less easily accessible.

"The Lancaster suffered teething problems with its bomb doors failing to close properly, the front-end jack moving faster than the jack at the rear, as a result of low oil temperature within the pipes that entered at the front and run the length of the bay.

"The Merlin XX engines, which powered both aircraft in the early days, also suffered their fair share of problems: water tended to leak through the top cylinder joint, which could cause the engine to catch fire.

"The Merlin 22 had a modified joint and the problem was solved, but the Merlin 28 – built in the US – also had a different diaphragm-operated carburettor, and the air intake was prone to icing up. This would cause the engines to 'surge' and, if not rectified quickly, the engines could be wrecked.

"Both aircraft suffered from 'swing' on take-off, and a severe crosswind could aggravate the situation and caused many accidents. It was also very difficult to train new pilots to land the Halifax well. She was a rather unforgiving aircraft; if you held off too high you didn't bounce, like you did in a Lancaster.

"You came down with a crunch, and could severely damage the aircraft. A good pilot, if he 'bounced' a Lancaster, could take off again, if full power was immediately applied. This was never the case with the Halifax."

WAR WINNERS

Humphrey eventually added to his two operational flights in 1942 with a full tour with 626 Squadron at Wickenby, Lincolnshire, in the winter of 1943-1944 at the height of the Battle of Berlin.

He was awarded the Distinguished Flying Cross and returned to instructor duties, seeing out the war as the Flight Engineer Leader of 1668 HCU at Balderton, Nottinghamshire.

Despite his views, Humphrey is happy to recognise the achievements of both aircraft, and their contribution to winning the war.

He also concedes that not every flight engineer would share his opinions:

"Ask the doyen of the flight engineer community, Flt Lt Ted Stocker DSO DFC, which aircraft he'd choose for a night 'op' to Cologne and he'd probably opt for the Halifax.

"Why? Because with your starboard wing ablaze, and the order given to bale out, you had a better chance of doing so safely from a Halifax!" ●

that could go wrong.

"There were five ways of getting the undercarriage down; the hydraulic power was supplemented by cylinders that stored air under pressure to be used in an emergency, so in theory we should have been safer, but in practice it just over-complicated matters.

"Some Halifax flight engineers will no doubt argue that you were fine if you knew your stuff, but it was a great deal to take in. Choosing the right course of action in an emergency, when you are under real pressure, is the difference between life and death.

LESS TO GO WRONG

"Everything about the Lancaster was easier: the fuel system was simpler, there were only three self-sealing fuel tanks in each wing. The

MAP MA

ABOVE
Lancaster TW652 over Kenya in August 1952.

Specially equipped Lancasters of 82 Squadron mapped much of West and Central Africa for the Ordnance Survey on behalf of the Colonial Office during the late 1940s. Thanks to the survival of one of 82's workhorses of that period, none other than the Battle of Britain Memorial Flight's PA474, another RAF map-maker, 683 Squadron, tends to get overlooked.

An additional unit was required to supplement 82 Squadron and to broaden the survey of areas of British influence in the Middle East. Having been disbanded in the Mediterranean in September 1945, 683 Squadron was selected to conduct the task.

At Fayid in the Suez Canal

Zone on November 1, 1950 Sqn Ldr Ian Lawson, an experienced reconnaissance pilot, began to re-form the new 683. As well as the aircrew, the unit had a full complement of engineers under Flt Lt Cantarus. As 683 was intended to fully deployable it had other trades, such as cooks and motor transport drivers. In all 683 Squadron comprised just over 100 men.

The unit had an establishment of four Lancaster PR.1s. The conversion involved the removal of the gun turrets, which were replaced by fairings. Much of the extensive glazing of the Lancaster's cockpit area was skinned with

aluminum to provide extra shade in hot climes.

In the bomb bay was an F49 fine-definition camera, weighing nearly 87lb (39kg). This had a 20in (50cm) lens and a magazine with 200 exposures of 9in x 9in film.

During its existence 683, Squadron used six PR.1s: PA379, PA394 'H', RA626 'S', TW652 'P', TW859 and TW916.

To help 683 achieve its roaming status, brand new Vickers Valetta C.1 VX498 was taken on charge. The twin-engined transport was used to move the detachments from base to base and provide support to the ground parties, often by air dropping water, fuel and rations.

SLOW AND METICULOUS

Deployments ventured throughout the Middle East and East Africa, often in conditions of great discomfort as cockpit temperatures regularly exceeded 49°C (120°F). The extreme heat and resulting turbulence challenged the skills of the pilots.

Accurate flying and navigation were of the greatest importance, especially on photo runs. Crews soon became expert in mastering the conditions, quickly building a good reputation in this specialised task.

A ground party would initially move to the survey area and

KERS

ROAMING AFRICA AND THE MIDDLE EAST ON PHOTO-SURVEY ASSIGNMENTS, THE LANCASTERS OF 683 SQUADRON WERE THE LAST TO SERVE THE RAF OPERATIONALLY. ANDREW THOMAS **EXPLAINS**

establish a radar beacon that became a datum for the aircraft. The Lancaster used the beacon as a 'hub' and flew around it at a fixed height, photographing a six-mile (9.6km) wide section of the ground. Following each sortie the area covered was added to the matrix and gradually as mosaic was built. It was slow, meticulous work.

AFRICAN VENTURE

A temporary move in February 1951 brought 683 back to Egypt's Canal Zone, this time at Kabrit; the unit staying there up to the end of April. While there, a shortage of beer and cigarettes was resolved by frequent training flights to Aden and Cyprus with the aircraft returning with bomb bay panniers full!

The next destination was Eastleigh in Nairobi, the capital of Kenya,

with the aircraft routing via Wadi Halfa, Omdurman, near Khartoum, and Juba. Primitive facilities en route meant the Lancasters had to be refuelled by hand pumps from barrels.

Over the next six months 683's Lancasters flew intensively over Central and East Africa. To broaden the areas covered single aircraft were detached to Livingstone in Northern Rhodesia (now Zambia) near the Victoria Falls and to Dar es Salaam in Tanganyika (now Tanzania). The detachment later moved to Entebbe, Uganda, for more mapping work.

The African survey period was not without incident, the worse occurring on June 24, 1951. The starboard engine failed on the Valetta and it made an emergency landing at Choma, between Livingstone and Lusaka. The

transport over-ran, the errant engine broke off its mounts and the undercarriage was whipped away. The Valetta was written off, but nobody was hurt.

One of the Lancasters had an incident at Livingstone when the pitot head was blocked by an insect. With no airspeed showing on the instruments, take-off had to be aborted resulting in slight damage when the tailplane struck a tree.

As well as cartographic and commercial benefit, 683's mapping efforts also had a military value. The images proved of great use during the campaign against the Mau Mau rebels in Kenya.

With the task in Central Africa completed, on September 24, 1951 the Lancasters returned to Kabrit. Soon, the men of 683 were off again, with a detachment ➡

BELOW
Four of 683 Squadron Lancaster PR.1s with the Valetta at Eastleigh, Kenya, in April 1951.

"...COCKPIT TEMPERATURES REGULARLY EXCEEDED 120°F. THE EXTREME HEAT AND RESULTING TURBULENCE CHALLENGED THE SKILLS OF THE PILOTS."

"MUCH OF THE WORK OF THE RAF IN THE MIDDLE EAST WAS PEACEKEEPING AND 'FLYING THE FLAG' AND 683's LARGE SILVER LANCASTERS MADE AN IMPRESSIVE VISUAL PRESENCE THROUGHOUT THE AREA."

to Shaibah, near Basra, to update surveys in southern Iraq and the northern Gulf area.

Another move for the itinerant squadron came in mid-December when it relocated to Khormaksar to chart the barren wilderness of the Aden Protectorate. One specific task was to survey a site for a radar beacon on a 6,200ft (1,890m) mountain top at the head of the so-called 'Murder Valley'.

Fg Off Goodyear led the ground team, which was initially supplied by air drops by the unit. The squadron also had a detachment manning a beacon in Yemen, where a supply drop nearly went badly wrong.

Two containers remained attached to the bomb bay shackles the equivalent of a 'hang up' on a bomber. The parachute rigging lines of the containers snagged around the tail. These acted like airbrakes, reducing the speed of the Lancaster to barely above the stall, while they were in a steep-sided wadi. Skilled flying, and more than a little luck, prevented this terrifying situation becoming a tragedy.

During the visit of Princess Elizabeth and the Duke of Edinburgh to Kenya, 683 was ordered to keep one aircraft at Juba and another at Wadi Halfa. Each was loaded with medical supplies

in the event of the Royal aircraft suffering a mishap.

Later, surveys were extended to British Somaliland and there were training flights to Asmara in Eritrea twice-weekly.

BURAIMI BLOCKADE
A detachment at Habbaniya in central Iraq resulted in the entire unit moving in on May 22, 1952. The recently promoted Sqn Ldr N N Ezekiel took command of 683 as the squadron began to concentrate on northern Iraq and Jordan.

When required, photographic reconnaissance flights were also flown to gather intelligence in the

LEFT
Valetta C.1 VX498 after coming to grief at Choma, Northern Rhodesia, April 24, 1951.

BELOW
A ground party of 683 Squadron at Roban, Iraq, recovering a container holding fresh meat and bread dropped by a Lancaster in April 1952.
ALL 683 SQUADRON
RECORDS UNLESS NOTED

increasingly unstable region. Much of the work of the RAF in the Middle East was peacekeeping and 'flying the flag' and 683's large silver Lancasters made an impressive visual presence throughout the area.

In early 1953 the unit began a high-priority plot of northern Persia that continued until July. It also mapped the southern end of the Gulf from a detachment based at Sharjah, including large parts of central Oman.

With much of the Ordnance Survey task completed, 683 Squadron was scheduled for disbandment at the end of July. For some years Saudi Arabia had cast covetous eyes on the oasis at Buraimi in Oman that was thought to have potential oil reserves. At the end of August 1952 a Saudi party

occupied the area and refused to withdraw.

After lengthy negotiations, the following March it was decided to initially mount an air blockade of the oasis to prevent supplies reaching the insurgents. Aircraft were to locate camel caravans that would then be intercepted by patrols of the Trucial Oman Levies and turned back.

With the Lancaster's lengthy endurance and the experience of 683's crews, the unit was considered ideal for patrols over the featureless desert. So instead of disbanding, two aircraft were detached to Sharjah. The detachment usually mounted one patrol over the area six days a week throughout August and September, concentrating on the distant approaches to Buraimi.

The patrols were flown at low level and the temperatures and severe turbulence often encountered were exhausting for the crews. Operational blockade patrols continued through October with the last one being flown in early November when the task was handed on to the Avro Anson C.19s of 1417 Flight.

During the blockade, 683's Lancasters flew more than 500 hours. The detachment returned to Habbaniya on November 13, 1953 where the Lancasters were prepared for return to Britain and it the unit disbanded on the 30th. The Buraimi stand-off had been the Lancaster's operational swansong with the RAF, it had fallen to 683 Squadron to bring to an end the Lancaster's illustrious frontline career. ●

MORE THAN FOUR

POST-WAR LANCASTERS AND LINCOLNS
WERE IN MUCH DEMAND AS ENGINE
TEST BEDS. MAXWELL EDISON
PRESENTS A PORTFOLIO

ABOVE
Sweden ordered a reconditioned Lancaster I from Avro that had been
strengthened to mount a turbojet in the bomb bay. Metropolitan-Vickers
1945-built Lancaster I RA805 was adapted by sister company Air Service
Training at Hamble and first flew in April 1951. With the Royal Swedish Air Force
serial 80001 it was fitted with a podded Svenska Turbinfabriks Dovern jet by
that July. This engine was intended to power the SAAB Lansen fighter, but was
cancelled in November 1952 in favour of the Rolls-Royce Avon. From 1954 the
Lancaster was used for trials of the de Havilland RM2 Ghost, but it was written
off in May 1956. KEY COLLECTION

RIGHT
Taken from the cabin of a DH Dominie, circa 1947, Lancaster II LL735 was part of
the National Gas Turbine Establishment fleet based at Bitteswell. It was fitted
with a Metropolitan-Vickers F2/4 Beryl turbojet in the tail,
with a large dorsal air intake. KEC

FAR RIGHT
Rolls-Royce converted Armstrong Whitworth-built Lincoln B.2 RF533 at Hucknall
in 1956 to take a Tyne turboprop in the nose. The Tyne was developed initially for
the Vickers Vanguard airliner. With the 'B Condition', or 'trade-plate' identity G-37-1
worn on the fuselage, the Lincoln caused a stir at the September 1956 Farnborough
airshow by performing on just the power of the Tyne. PETER GREEN COLLECTION

"ROLLS-ROYCE CONVERTED ARMSTRONG WHITWORTH-BUILT LINCOLN B.2 RF533 AT HUCKNALL IN 1956 TO TAKE A TYNE TURBOPROP IN THE NOSE."

LEFT
Built by Armstrong Whitworth, 'Tiger Force' schemed Lancaster III TW911 was issued to sister company Armstrong Siddeley and converted with a pair of Python turboprops with contra-rotating propellers in the outer engine positions. Testing, for the Westland Wyvern shipborne fighter programme, was carried out from 1949 to 1952. ASM

RIGHT
Lancaster III, ND784, was converted as one of a small number of Mk.VIs for trials of Rolls-Royce Merlin 85s with annular cowlings as used on the Lincoln. It was employed as a test-bed for Power Jets and later Armstrong Siddeley, operating from Bitteswell. It was fitted with an ASX turbojet mounted in the bomb bay during 1946 and from 1947 to 1951 with a Mamba turboprop in the nose (illustrated). ARMSTRONG SIDDELEY

RIGHT
Bristol converted Lincoln B.2 SX972 to test out the Proteus turboprop, destined for its Britannia airliner, in 1949. It is illustrated at Filton, overflying the one-off Bristol Brabazon airliner, circa 1950. BRISTOL

INSIDE

Resident at the former Lancaster station at East Kirkby, Lincolnshire, former French Navy Mk.VII 'Just Jane' has for many years delighted hundreds of veterans and enthusiasts by providing taxi rides. Countless more have gloried in the many special events run by the Lincolnshire Aviation Heritage Centre 'starring' the Lancaster. Now there are plans to take NX611 back into the air and public help is vital for this £3 million project.

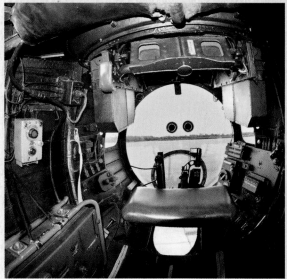

JOB

DARREN HARBAR REVEALS THE INTERIOR OF 'JUST JANE'

TOP LEFT
Looking forward: the radar station, radio operator's desk and the cockpit.

TOP RIGHT
The rear gun turret, with the tailplane carry-through in the foreground.

ABOVE
The bomb aimer's 'office'.

RIVETING SUPPORT FOR 'JUST JANE'

During the winter of 2016-2017 major works have been carried out on the Lincolnshire Aviation Heritage Centre's Lancaster NX611 'Just Jane' with huge strides made towards restoring her to airworthy condition. LAHC's Andrew Panton notes that: "The goal of 'Just Jane' becoming only the third airworthy Lancaster in the world feels closer than ever before."

The current work amounts to an investment in the region of £250,000. With such a significant financial input LAHC has launched the Rivet Club to support the East Kirkby-based Lancaster. For a monthly donation, members will have special access to news updates and the weekly overhaul reports not otherwise available. Andrew says: "We really hope the public will support our work and really get on board with the aim of restoring 'Just Jane' to her rightful airworthy condition." For more details about how you can get involved take a look at: www.lincsaviation.co.uk

LEGACY

JONATHAN GARRAWAY EXAMINES HOW THE LANCASTER BECAME THE FOUNDER OF A FAMILY

Designer Roy Chadwick was a past master at taking an airframe and making it work hard. Different engines, new roles, aerodynamic tweaks were all investigated and, if found to be advantageous, a new variant was born and the family extended.

He started with the Avro 504, the father of all trainers which was manufactured for 20 years in a bewildering number of versions into the early 1930s. The Anson capitalised on this system, indeed from its very beginning in 1935 it morphed from VIP shuttle to maritime patroller. It was in production all the way through to 1952 and in that time it changed in almost every way except for its general layout.

With problematical engines forced upon him, Chadwick triumphed over an overly-demanding specification to create the Manchester twin-engined bomber, which first flew in 1939. For a company that had made its name in training and, more recently, general-

from acceptable, even in war. The bomber could have been consigned to history at that point, but Roy knew that the design was sound and Rolls-Royce Merlin engines would turn its fortunes around. The answer was the Manchester III, renamed the Lancaster, which turned out to be Bomber Command's weapon of choice. Like Chadwick's most successful ventures, the Lancaster spawned its own dynasty.

ACROSS THE PENNINES

As related in the feature 75 Lancs, the Canadians were the first to exploit the Lancaster's roomy fuselage and long range with the XPP passenger transport. Refined by Roy Chadwick this led to the Lancastrian which helped to pioneer intercontinental services in the late 1940s. (Born and bred in Lancashire, Roy must have enjoyed – and perhaps influenced – the new airliner's name.)

The Lancastrian was a relatively simple undertaking. Prior to its

purpose twins, the Manchester was a huge leap in complexity, both in terms of systems, powerplant structure and in the planning and logistics to mass produce it.

In testing and service the Manchester had performance and reliability deficiencies that were far

conception, Roy had come up with the most radical member of the species. For this he took the well-proven powerplant, wings, undercarriage and tail 'feathers' and married them to a brand new, ultra-wide, fuselage.

What would the new machine be called? The choice lay on the other side of the Pennines, it was to be called York.

The RAF desperately needed a high-capacity transport, but the Lancaster remained the priority for Avro. On the proviso that it was not to detract from its bomber ➔

RIGHT
Tracing its lineage all the way back to the Manchester, the prototype Shackleton, VW126, in 1949. AVRO

BELOW
The prototype Lincoln, PW925, in the summer of 1944. KEC

forebear, work on the York was permitted on a private venture basis by the Ministry of Aircraft Production. Having signed off the plans, the experimental shop finished the prototype, LV626, just five months later; 'Sam' Brown taking it on its maiden flight from Ringway – now Manchester Airport – on July 5, 1942. Testing went well; externally the only major change was the addition of a middle fin on the tail.

On the Lancaster, the wing was fitted to the fuselage at 'shoulder' height, on the York it was at the top of the fuselage. This meant that the wing carry-through structure hardly interfered with the capacity of the box-like fuselage. This position also allowed the floor to be much closure to the ground, greatly facilitating the loading of cargo.

Including one example assembled in Canada, York production totalled an impressive 258 units and ran from 1943 to 1948. Initially completed at Woodford, from late 1945 the transport truly became a Yorkshireman when the assembly line moved to Yeadon – today's Leeds-Bradford Airport. The bulk served with the RAF, but airlines – including British Overseas Airways Corporation, British South American Airlines – also ordered Yorks.

The type found an eager second-hand market with commercial operators, increasingly as a freighter. The last-ever flight by a York took place on October 9, 1964 when the former Skyways G-AGNV was ferried to the Skyfame Museum at Staverton, Glos. Today, this machine is displayed within the National Cold War Exhibition, part of the RAF Museum Cosford, Shropshire.

'SUPER LANCASTER'
By the time of D-Day, June 6, 1944, strategic planning was already in hand about how the war against Japan would be concluded. Bomber Command was to contribute what became known as 'Tiger Force', initially equipped with Lancasters

modified for use in the Far East. A more powerful and bigger Lancaster was required and Roy Chadwick turned his design team to making a 'super' version.

This programme was at first designated Lancaster IV and V with Rolls-Royce or Packard-built Merlins, respectively. As much of the Lancaster was included in the new type as possible in order to speed development and the resulting bomber's heritage was obvious.

Span was extended from the Lancaster I's 102ft 0in (31m) to 120ft 0in and length grew from 69ft 4in to 78ft 3in. The Lancaster's Merlin 22s were rated at 1,280hp (954kW) while the new type had Merlin 85s of 1,750hp. All-up weight increased dramatically, from 49,950lb (22,657kg) to 82,000lb.

Just as the Manchester III needed a new name – Lancaster – to emphasise how different it was from its predecessor, so the Lancaster IV and V had to adopt a new label. Keeping to the county town theme, it was called Lincoln, reflecting the region from which so many Lancasters were despatched.

Test pilot 'Sam' Brown was at the helm for the maiden flight of the

prototype, PW925, from Ringway on June 9, 1944. In the same month that Japan surrendered, August 1945, the first Lincolns were issued to 57 Squadron at East Kirkby, Lincolnshire. Lincolns went on to be Bomber Command's post-war mainstay until the early 1950s when the jet-powered English Electric Canberra took over.

In total, 529 Lincolns were ordered for the RAF and a small number served with the Argentine Air Force (RAAF). A single example was built in Canada and Australia manufactured the type under licence for its air force; the Government Aircraft Factory at Fishermens Bend, Melbourne, making 54 Mk.30s.

SLEDGEHAMMERS
While the Lincoln did not see action in World War Two, it was used to combat guerrilla forces in Kenya and Malaya. Based at Eastleigh, Nairobi, detachments of Lincolns attacked the Mau Mau 1953 to 1954. The big bombers had a limited effect in this conflict, being described as

"...PART NUMBERS CAN BE FOUND WITHIN THE STRUCTURE OF THE SHACKLETON THAT CAN BE TRACED BACK TO THE DAYS OF THE MANCHESTER. ASTOUNDING DESIGN LONGEVITY, JUST AS ROY CHADWICK WOULD HAVE WANTED IT."

"like using a sledgehammer to crack a walnut" by an armourer from 100 Squadron.

Famously understated as the 'Emergency', the struggle with communist insurgents in Malaya was waged, ultimately to success, from 1948 to 1960. Detachments of Lincolns were introduced to the region in March 1950, based at Tengah, Singapore. The first raid was staged on the 26th.

Terrorist camps and supply dumps located deep in the dense and vast Malayan jungle were more appropriate targets for the 'sledgehammers'. The unsophisticated 1,000lb bomb was used to devastating effect, each Lincoln carrying 14 in its huge weapons bay. Detonations within a wooded area generated shockwaves and countless wooden shards causing considerable damage to the makeshift guerrilla installations.

When conditions permitted, up to five Lincolns flying in close formation at relatively low level could inflict massive damage to manpower, materiel and morale. These tactics forced the enemy to abandon large bases and disperse its forces into smaller groups, greatly reducing its combat ability.

From June 1950 RAAF Lincolns arrived at Tengah to take part in operations. The RAF withdrew the type from March 1955 when Canberras took over. The RAAF kept its Lincolns in theatre until February 1956.

First appearing in 1951 a number of Australian Lincolns were built or converted with forward fuselages extended by 6ft 6in to act as interim maritime patrollers. The RAAF Lincoln force was retired in June 1961. The Last RAF examples were employed by 151 Squadron at Watton, Norfolk, and the final trio flew a farewell formation on March 12, 1963. One of the participants was RF398, now on display at the RAF Museum Cosford, Shropshire.

40 YEARS OF SERVICE
Much of the wing structure, powerplant and systems of the Lincoln were utilised in the ill-fated Tudor airliner programme – see *Biplane to Delta* on page 6. A Mk.III Lincoln for air-sea rescue and maritime patrol was initiated by Chadwick and his team, but this was sidelined in favour of a more comprehensive solution.

A shorter, but more capacious, fuselage was mated to a Lincoln wing, with four 2,450hp Rolls-Royce Griffon 57As driving counter-rotating propellers. Before he died in the Tudor 2 prototype in August 1947, Roy was supervising mock-ups of the crew positions on this project, which was to emerge as the last Avro 'heavy', the long-serving Shackleton.

Jimmy Orrell carried out the inaugural flight of the prototype, VW126, on March 9, 1949 and the RAF received its first Shackleton GR.1 (later MR.1) in April 1951. Production totalled 178 in three major variants; the last coming off the line in 1959.

Just as the Lancaster gave its wing to the York and the Lincoln passed its on to the Shackleton, so Avro's maritime patroller came to the aid of a fellow member of the Hawker Siddeley Group, Armstrong Whitworth. The wing structure was adopted for the Argosy four-turboprop airlifter, which appeared in January 1959.

As a stopgap, an airborne early warning version, the Shackleton AEW.2 was created. The first conversion, WL745, flew at Woodford on September 30, 1971 and it was followed by 11 more. The fleet soldiered on until July 1, 1991 – Shackleton had clocked a staggering 40 years of service.

I'm reliably informed that part numbers can be found within the structure of the Shackleton that can be traced back to the days of the Manchester. Astounding design longevity, just as Roy Chadwick would have wanted it. ●

TOP
The prototype York, LV626, in August 1942.

ABOVE
Armstrong Whitworth-built Lincoln B.2 RF562 of 230 Operational Conversion Unit, Scampton, 1950.
PETE WEST

"THE LANCASTER SURPASSED ALL OTHER TYPES OF HEAVY BOMBER... I USED THE LANCASTER ALONE FOR THOSE ATTACKS WHICH INVOLVED THE DEEPEST PENETRATION INTO GERMANY AND WERE, CONSEQUENTLY, THE MOST DANGEROUS. I WOULD SAY THIS TO THOSE WHO PLACED THAT SHINING SWORD IN OUR HANDS: WITHOUT YOUR GENIUS AND EFFORTS WE COULD NOT HAVE PREVAILED, FOR I BELIEVE THAT THE LANCASTER WAS THE GREATEST SINGLE FACTOR IN WINNING THE WAR."

ACM SIR ARTHUR HARRIS TO SIR ROY DOBSON OF AVRO, DECEMBER 1945

Bomber Command re-enactors with the Lincolnshire Aviation Heritage Centre's 'Just Jane'.
DARREN HARBAR PHOTOGRAPHY

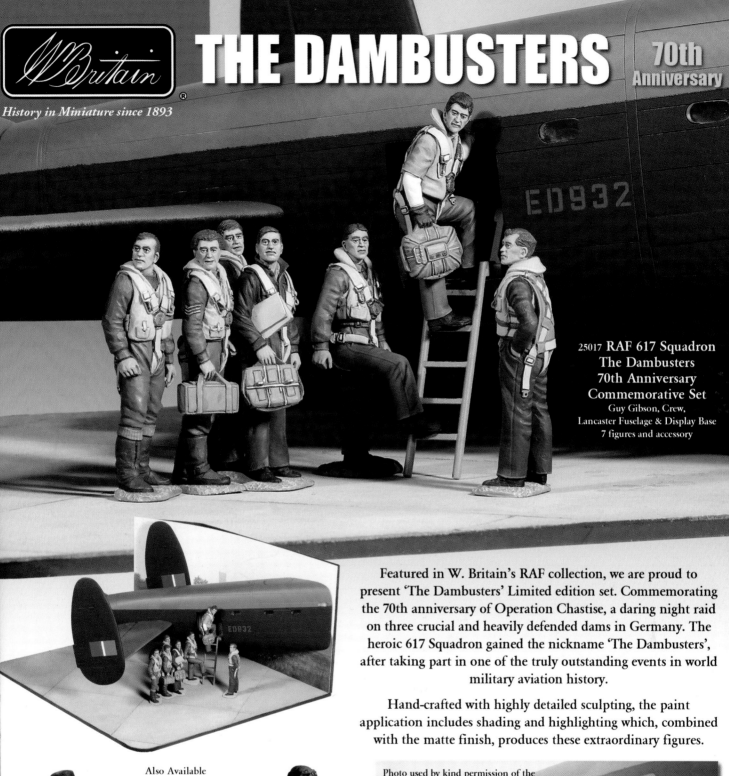

W. Britain
THE DAMBUSTERS 70th Anniversary

History in Miniature since 1893

25017 RAF 617 Squadron The Dambusters 70th Anniversary Commemorative Set
Guy Gibson, Crew, Lancaster Fuselage & Display Base
7 figures and accessory

Featured in W. Britain's RAF collection, we are proud to present 'The Dambusters' Limited edition set. Commemorating the 70th anniversary of Operation Chastise, a daring night raid on three crucial and heavily defended dams in Germany. The heroic 617 Squadron gained the nickname 'The Dambusters', after taking part in one of the truly outstanding events in world military aviation history.

Hand-crafted with highly detailed sculpting, the paint application includes shading and highlighting which, combined with the matte finish, produces these extraordinary figures.

Also Available

LEFT - 25023 Prime Minister Winston Churchill No.1
1 Piece Set

RIGHT - 25019 RAF Fighter Pilot 1943 with Faithful Companion
2 Piece Set

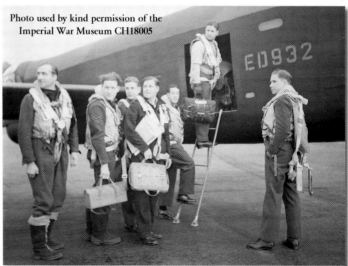

Photo used by kind permission of the Imperial War Museum CH18005

1:30 Scale
Steeped in history, revered for quality

To view the full range of W. Britain die-cast figures please visit
www.wbritain.net

BACHMANN EUROPE Plc
Model, Collect & Create